Get Rich
In The Deep End

Get Rich In The Deep End / Brent Weaver

ISBN-13: 979-8-692697-69-1

Get Rich In The Deep End

Commit to your niche, own your market, and audaciously scale your agency.

Brent Weaver
with Aaron Wrixon

DEDICATION

To Emily, my wife, my partner, my reason for stepping up.

To my boys—you're the light of my life.

To my parents, for encouraging me to chart my own path.

To my brother, the relentless teacher.

To Marc, reminding me to love the process.

And to Wrixon—this was the most fun I've had working, ever.

TABLE OF CONTENTS

PROLOGUE
Heather Has a Problem.. 13

CHAPTER ONE
An Introduction to "Getting Rich In The Deep End"................. 21

CHAPTER TWO
Heather Meets Her Mentor... 35

CHAPTER THREE
The 5-A Framework™... 46

CHAPTER FOUR
Heather Chooses Her Audience... 60

CHAPTER FIVE
The First A—Audience... 68

CHAPTER SIX
Heather Builds Awareness... 91

CHAPTER SEVEN
The Second A—Awareness.. 101

CHAPTER EIGHT
Heather Learns How to Attract Her Audience......................... 123

CHAPTER NINE
The Third A—Attract 131

CHAPTER TEN
Heather Builds Authority 164

CHAPTER ELEVEN
The Fourth A—Authority 171

CHAPTER TWELVE
Heather Acquires New Leads 198

CHAPTER THIRTEEN
The Fifth A—Acquire 206

CHAPTER FOURTEEN
Heather Gives Her Talk 230

CONCLUSION
A New Way 243

EPILOGUE
Heather Comes Full Circle 249

About the Author 252

Notes 253

AUTHOR'S NOTE

As we prepared to publish this book, I couldn't help but wonder how readers would perceive it, given everything going on in the world. Was the strategy of niching still the right thing to do? Was the age of specialization over? Do people want experts anymore?

In late March of 2020, I was on the phone with an agency owner (not yet a client), and he said, "I'm so thankful I'm not niched right now–I feel like being a generalist makes me recession-proof." My heart sank. While I had internally questioned how these world events would impact our work, no one had outright said this statement to me. I immediately started to question everything we'd been working on over the last couple of years.

The days immediately before that conversation were immensely hard. I had taken dozens of client calls, hosted emergency workshops, and threw out a lot of what we'd been working on earlier in the year.

We had agency owner clients who had lost a large portion of their client base overnight. Some of the hardest-hit markets like restaurants, hotels, travel, and touch-based businesses like gyms and medical practices faced decimation.

I was at a crossroads. Either throw everything out and create something new or pick up the principles taught in this book and see how they work during the Great Reset of 2020.

My team and I went into serve overdrive. We figured out ways to help our clients mitigate cancellations. We helped them to pivot their messaging. Iterate on their offers to keep them relevant.

We stood on the 5A's taught in this book and encouraged our clients to get back to their markets' fundamentals. Get even more explicit about the Audience you serve. Identify Awareness channels that you can use to get your message to this Audience. Talk about the three to five top problems your market is experiencing right now that you can solve to Attract more leads to your door. Establish your Authority by sharing proof of results and case studies. And build a clear path to a conversation to Acquire ideal clients like never before.

What happened over the following months was an incredible rollercoaster that I'm so thankful to have witnessed.

One client who lost his entire marketing engine to conference and event cancellations–he spoke on two stages a month in his market–pivoted to virtual workshops and helped his market find their way during a crisis. He leveraged all of the relationships he had built over the last 18 months in his niche to promote his workshops and recently delivered his first paid, self-hosted event that led to 17 new qualified leads wanting proposals.

Another client helped their small business clients apply for government grants to help the businesses build online stores to take their struggling retail businesses into the e-commerce revolution. He gave hope to companies that would have otherwise shut down and could not afford to pivot–this service mindset helped him win more business in 2020 than any prior year for his agency.

One of my hardest hit clients does work with hotels in the Caribbean. His agency lost 50% of his clients overnight. Since March, he's hosted a dozen or more webinars and workshops helping hotels figure out new ways to bring in revenue and market their properties during lockdowns. This work has helped him get more leads in the last five months than during the previous five years combined. While his business is only back to 80% of what it once was, he cut 50% of his expenses while continuing to get his clients great results. The other day, he said that COVID-19 was the best thing that ever happened to his business.

Many generalists weren't forced to pivot their businesses. They weren't forced to innovate and come up with new solutions, offers, or packages. They weren't forced to lay off staff or figure out how to do way more with way less. And while that might seem a good place to be in the short-term, long-term, I believe it will be a costly lesson as they are left in the dust by the results that niched specialists are able to get their clients.

Here are five observations of the last five months:

1. The playing field has been leveled.

If you've been waiting on the sidelines to niche and own your market, now is a great time. Many of the experts of yesterday are still trying to figure out what works in this new economy.

2. Those with market authority have a leg up.

If you have a list and Audience, the last five months have created unprecedented opportunities for you to stand out as your market leader. There is a massive leadership vacuum in the world today–if you share with your Audience what is working, more people will follow you than ever before.

3. Marketing your agency is more important than ever.

For many, referrals and word of mouth dried up when Covid-19 hit, which hobbled many agencies' ability to sign new clients and keep the lights on. Recession-proof your business by building two or three proven marketing engines.

4. Just because you have a bunch of clients in a niche doesn't mean you own your market.

Agencies that were "niched" but didn't have any market authority, lists, or following experienced challenges hard to overcome. They lost clients but were unable to quickly attract new clients who were thriving in the niche they served because they couldn't quickly email their list, publish content easily absorbed, or capture interested leads.

5. The new economy is a *winner take all* marketplace.

As the internet, social media, and technology continue to advance at breakneck speeds, market needs will become increasingly more specialized. If it's not already difficult to operate as a generalist, over the next ten years, I believe it will become close to impossible to run a highly profitable and scalable agency as one.

Markets like restaurants, gyms, dental practices, and even lawyers became a lot more complicated overnight. Advertising and marketing platforms are becoming increasingly intricate and nuanced.

Imagine yourself in the shoes of a successful restaurant owner when faced with the question of which web agency to hire:

a) The generalist web pro that has developed some great looking websites for various businesses or

b) The restaurant specialist who has helped over one hundred restaurants launch online orders for delivery and curbside business with a proven track record of increasing sales by 125% on average– and has proprietary frameworks and software to speed up the launch by cutting 75% from development timelines.

Swap the specific restaurant jargon out for any other market's particular problems and desired outcomes, and you get the idea. The specialist will win the day ninety-nine times out of one hundred.

This book is not just about specialization, but about you building a practice of publishing, speaking, and advertising to your market about your unique skills, knowledge, and services so you can create a highly profitable and scalable agency business.

That's why, even in the new economy, you need to Get Rich in the Deep End.

 **Most businesses target everyone so they end up owning nothing.**

Heather Has a Problem

To the casual observer, nothing at EMA—Everyday Marketing Agency—seemed out of place.

Hip letterpress posters hung on the walls, accenting the bright and dynamic decor. The open floor plan buzzed with energy. Team members drank Red Bull and worked either head-down, focused on the intricacies of pixels and positioning, or chatting and collaborating with broad smiles on their faces. And had you visited EMA that day, you might not have noticed anything amiss.

Among the other agencies in town, EMA had always been a leader, and its owner, Heather Carlyle, was "the belle of the ball." Other agencies in town often felt jealous, only wishing their companies could be as successful as hers. The award-winning work, the A-List clients, the cool office—Heather had it all. And when you visited EMA, it certainly seemed that way.

On this day, however—if you looked hard enough—you'd find something troubling just beyond the foosball table. There, past the fishbowl conference room, on the opposite side of a glass door, Heather was in a state of panic.

She had just read an email from her next big "fish." The lead was supposed to have been signing on to a massive project, but in fact, they had just informed her they were delaying their planned project indefinitely. That's when Heather realized she had only one other deal in her pipeline—and that, in just a few weeks, the agency's current work would wrap up.

Heather looked out across the office at her team—each member working hard, oblivious to the pressing crisis her business was now facing. *"If they knew the truth,"* she thought, *"they'd all run for the exit. I need to solve this problem fast or I'll need to cut at least a third of them. Maybe more."*

 ## Trying to grow a business on word of mouth is called Hope *Marketing*.

Truth be told, Heather had built her business almost exclusively on referrals and word of mouth. That approach had worked in the past. Since launching EMA a decade ago, after leaving a soul-sucking corporate marketing gig, Heather had always had that "next" project. Referrals just happened.

But now they were almost dried up. Heather opened her browser and pulled up the EMA website. A quick look at her blog showed it had been eighteen months since the last post.

Heather frowned and fired off a quick email to one of her team members and told him to write something on responsive web design. "Reference the launch we just did for Amy," she wrote. Her hunch was that the site they had just finished for her longtime friend—a successful business coach and author—would play well in a case study.

But deep down, Heather was afraid she was grasping at straws. Her phone buzzed. Coincidentally, Amy was on the line. Heather had completely forgotten she'd promised Amy that they'd attend a local restaurateur event together.

But she wasn't dressed for networking! Heather looked down at her jeans and sighed. "I guess I should change my clothes. Because I needed one 'more' thing to do."

Heather paused in front of her closet. She knew she didn't have time to dawdle, but she couldn't help thinking…

What if she wore the Versace top she bought in Florence last month? It was certainly attention-getting. In fact, it could probably be used to stop traffic—it included every color of the rainbow and was emblazoned with *Vogue* magazine covers.

It was like nothing else in Heather's wardrobe. Truthfully, she had no idea why she had bought it; in a moment of wild abandon, she'd simply decided she had to have the thing. Paid a pretty penny for it, too, but at the time, she had been convinced it was worth it.

Heather blinked and shook her head. What was she thinking? This was a networking event, not a cocktail party. With a sigh, she pulled a black blazer and pants from the closet and quickly got changed.

"If only people in the States knew fashion like the Italians," **she thought,** *"business would certainly be a heck of a lot more fun."*

The Event

As Heather walked into the event, she did a double take. At the convention center entrance was a sign welcoming guests and promoting the afternoon's guest speaker—Jake Wardholl.

"Of all the people," Heather thought. Jake was Heather's competitor. And a college classmate of both her and Amy.

The picture showed Jake in an upscale restaurant kitchen, gripping a large knife and holding a serving dish with an iPad and iPhone on it. In giant block letters below the photo were Jake's name and the slogan, "The World's #1 Restaurant Marketing Guru."

Heather hadn't spoken to Jake in a year or more, but she was still surprised to see him so focused on restaurants. She certainly didn't remember him talking about moving in this direction. Making her way into the main hall, Heather spotted Amy.

"Gosh, Amy, can you believe that Jake is their keynote speaker? Last we saw him, he was working some huge corporate accounts."

Before Amy could respond, the emcee began his pleasantries from the stage, so the two women quickly found seats and sat down. The emcee welcomed the audience and introduced Jake with a rap sheet of accolades and accomplishments related to restaurant marketing. Then Jake entered, wearing a cheesy grin and the same oversized chef hat as on the entrance poster.

"I want to set everyone straight here," he opened.

"I'm not a chef. I can hardly pronounce 'mise en place.'" Jake added his southern drawl to the cooking jargon and tilted his head as if to invoke the audience's approval. Heather cringed, but his listeners erupted in laughter.

Jake went on. "I still don't fully understand why you season the pan and not the steak. I have no idea what FF&E you need to open a restaurant. And not one of you in this room would—or should—let me manage your food or wine buying. Trust me, I'm no solminer." Again, at his stagey butchering of the word *sommelier*, the audience let out a loud laugh.

"Is Jake for real? I can't believe they're buying this junk," **Heather thought.** *"And what on earth does any of this have to do with marketing? I guess I'm not going to learn much at this event after all."*

Jake continued. "But what I do know is that your restaurant might be just a few slow nights away from closing. Every week, a new hotspot opens up in this city, vying for your customers' hard-earned dollars.

"I know that employee turnover is killing the consistency of your marketing. I know that QSRs are pulling the four-person family, your bread and butter, away from your tables. And I know that while you might not feel like you have to market your restaurant today, there will come a time when being 'new' or 'cool' won't be enough to pay your ten-year lease.

"But the good news is, I have a solution. Today I'm going to walk you through the Rapid Restaurant Growth Formula—my proven framework to help you create the marketing systems your business needs to get more hungry mouths at your restaurant's tables."

Heather tuned out. Clearly, she wasn't the target for Jake's talk. Her mind wandered back to the last deal in her pipeline. She needed to close it if EMA were going to live to fight another day.

Then she remembered that the friend who referred her was on another team at the same company. Heather pulled out her phone and tapped an email to her inside source, looking to get a pulse on where the approver was in their decision-making process. One email led to another, and soon Heather was lost to the demands of her inbox.

But she was shaken out of her distraction when it seemed like the entire audience pulled out their phones, too, in unison. She looked up and saw a web address on the presentation screen. Jake was giving away his Rapid Restaurant Growth Formula™ and offering a sixty-minute strategy session to review the completed document for all attendees—a service he usually charged for.

With a sinking feeling, Heather realized that Jake had just set himself up for at least fifty leads.

What did she miss?

As Jake's talk concluded, Heather looked at Amy and blurted out, "I need a drink. Pronto."

Amy chuckled. "No need to convince me. There's a reception out in the main hall." A few minutes later, as Heather relaxed with a glass of chardonnay, Amy thanked her.

"The work you guys did on my website is incredible. I can't tell you how awesome it is to finally be able to make some passive income as a coach selling my online course. I don't know how EMA pulled that off, but we're getting new customers every day."

Heather started to reply. "Well, Amy, at EMA we're all about—"

"Heather! Amy!" A man's familiar Southern accent called from over their shoulders, jolting the two women. Jake walked up and folded them into a group hug like some kind of impromptu college reunion. Amy teased Jake, "Where's the chef hat? What—you don't wear that all the time?"

Jake replied, "Aw shucks, that's just a bit of showbiz. I'm going out on the town later, and it works like magic when you want to start up a conversation. But seriously, how are the two of you all doing?"

Clearly, Heather had more on her mind. "Busy, busy, Jake, but listen—what happened with your big corporate clients? I'm a bit surprised to see you here."

"Heather, can you keep a secret?" Jake began. "Between you and me and Amy here, our agency almost folded about a year ago. I had a bit of an awakening, to say the least.

"One day, the referrals just disappeared. Nothing but tumbleweeds. And I realized how little control I had over how we earned business.

"Now, this wasn't the first time it happened, either, but a year ago things got so bad I had to lay off a bunch of my team. Loud as a rooster—it was a wake-up call.

"I had to make a change. Not all of us are as lucky as you over at EMA," Jake smiled and clinked Heather's wine glass with his Coke.

Heather was uncomfortable. "Do you mean niching down? I would never do that. Like I always say—if they can pay the bill, they can be my client."

Jake replied with a slow nod. "Now, I feel you, Heather. I know what you're saying. And I used to think the same way, but my business was gone faster than a toupee in a hurricane.

"And I was a deer in the headlights. Paralyzed. We had no leads, and I had no idea what to do next. I lost a couple of 'sure things,' and the floor fell out from underneath me."

Heather looked wide-eyed. "Wow. I had no idea. Everything looked so good from the outside."

Jake tapped a finger to his temple. "My clients call that the front of the house—like the part of the restaurant where the customers eat. But the back of the house was a disaster. Know what saved me? By chance, I happened to go to a conference like this one. I heard a fella speak about this stuff. Felt like he was inside my head. So, I hired him."

 **Scaling your business on referrals is the same as sitting by the phone waiting for it to ring.**

"Listen, Heather. I know that specializing, or niching down, or whatever you want to call it makes you about as nervous as a long-tailed cat in a room full of rocking chairs. But if you ever change your mind, here's the business card I got from the guy at the conference. He made a big difference for me when we worked together.

"I'm sure leads aren't a problem for you, but if you find yourself in the situation I was in someday, you're gonna want this number."

Jake pulled a crumpled business card from his bag and passed it to Heather.

She glanced at it—*"Own Your Market"*™—and politely put it in her pocket.

"Thanks, Jake," she said, "but it's time for me to head out. Great talk, buddy. Amy, I'll speak to you tomorrow. We have a couple of loose ends to wrap up with your project. Nice to see you both."

As she walked to the exit, Heather checked her phone for new emails and found one from her "inside source" at her last lead's company. What she read sent her reeling.

"Heather, I'm not sure why they haven't told you yet. I probably shouldn't be the one to say so, but the team chose a different agency for the project. So sorry."

Heather stifled a gasp and kept walking so Jake and Amy couldn't see her fighting back the tears.

CHAPTER ONE

An Introduction to "Getting Rich In The Deep End"

Have you ever said these words?

"I don't have a particular industry or market I target."

"I have a niche I want to specialize in, but I don't have any clients in it."

"I have a few different niches I focus on."

"I don't even know where to start with this whole 'niching' thing!"

Then you're in the right place.

At best, many agencies and professional services businesses act like they *rent* their markets—paying for access and dipping in as necessary, without any permanent commitment.

Other businesses visit markets here and there like tourists traveling through for occasional day-trips. These people then head back to their cozy "homes" without acquiring any specialty or expertise.

But renters and tourists never get to the real essence of a market. They are stuck on the surface-level experiences. They're at least better than generalists with no defined market, or dreamers who have ideas about what they want to do but no traction or first steps. But there is, in fact, a fifth level of involvement in a market:

To review:

1. Outsiders have no market, no niche, no intention.

2. Dreamers want to specialize in a market but have taken no action.

3. Tourists show up in markets occasionally, but with generalist skills.

4. Renters work in a few markets, here and there, as opportunities present themselves.

Owners are inseparable from their market—and nearly synonymous with it, as a result. Owners aren't tourists. They set up residence. They become locals, learn the language, and acquire citizenship. Owners care. Take a look at Exhibit 1 to see the differences between a tourist mindset and an owner mindset:

Exhibit 1

MARKET "TOURIST"	MARKET "OWNER"
Market Small business and nonprofits Hundres of millions of possibilities worldwide	**Market** IT service companies in the US with fewer than 20 staff About 20k businesses
Homepage "Your go-to creative studio for design and development"	**Homepage** "Win New Customers with Strategic MSP Marketing"
Tagline "Web Design, Web Development, Brand Identity, Product Design"	**Tagline** "We help MSPs and B2B IT service providers win new customers through strategic digital marketing"

Marketing Activities	Marketing Activities
☐ Random, Disconnected ☐ Post completed projects to portfolio ☐ Pay for membership in directories ☐ Search for jobs on sites like Upwork ☐ Occasional marketing produces sporadic results	☐ Strategic, focused ☐ Publish authority articles on high traffic websites in niche ☐ Retarget traffic on FB and AdWords back to additional content and calls to action ☐ Systemized marketing is in place that converts targeted traffic to scheduled calls automatically
Results ☐ Business survives on referrals ☐ No clarity about marketing activities ☐ Every client is different, breaking processes ☐ Building trust and credibility with every client requires a substantial investment of time and energy ☐ No predictability around leads and sales	**Results** ☐ Pipeline of leads ensures sales are always happening ☐ Growing email list to nurture long term ☐ Clear marketing activities ☐ Incoming client have consistent problem sets, making processes and productized services easier to build ☐ Authority status helps prospects trust the agency on the first interaction ☐ Business is predictable and can be influenced by growth levers

Many of us can more closely identify with the kind of business you see on the left, but we'd all probably prefer to have the results of the agency on the right (even if you don't know what MSP stands for).

The agency on the right *owns* its market. They understand who their customers are, and what those customers' problems are, and they proudly speak to them and their issues with a strategic focus.

The truth is, very few businesses ever make their way up to *owning* a market. Most languish at one of the other levels—outsider, dreamer, tourist, or renter. Now, you might be thinking that's fine. "I don't want to *own* a market! That sounds possessive. Greedy, even." But owning a market is *not* about making that market your *property*. Because there are two definitions of the verb *own*:[1]

1. Have (something) as one's own; possess.

2. Admit or acknowledge that something is the case or that one feels a certain way.

This book is about the second definition, so it concentrates on the relationship your market has with your identity and focus as a business. By owning your market, you're admitting to yourself that you feel committed to it. That you owe it to your market to serve it as well as you can.

In other words, "owning your market"—in the way I mean— is about your mindset. You stop "dipping a toe in," keeping the door open to other niches and opportunities. You quit traveling through a market as a tourist. Instead, you jump into the deep end and allow your market to seep into your bones.

You get comfortable shouting your market position from the rooftops and letting the world *know* how you feel. You're okay with the idea that there is a particular customer you serve—and if someone isn't that type, they aren't a good fit. You allow the identity of the market to wash over you, no longer forced to switch between a dozen different identities.

 **There's a reason heart and brain surgeons make a lot more money than a family doctor.**

When you make a decision to jump into the deep end, you are making the choice to niche and own your market, you transform and simplify your business life. You're no longer trying to be everything to everyone. Instead, you become a pillar of your community. You go from outsider to insider. And this happens:

- When people ask what you do, you clearly and comfortably state your market and who you serve.
- Your website loudly proclaims your market focus.
- You regularly publish content for, speak to, and evangelize to your market.
- You have an audience built within your market.
- You have a deep understanding of your market's pains and problems.

Owning is when you think, "This is my market. I need to act accordingly," instead of continuing to keep one foot out the door.

Instead of considering things on the surface, you put down roots and invest in more long-term relationships. You're no longer concerned about short-term blips but about solving deep, valuable issues for your audience.

Can you see now why market ownership is not a bad thing, but actually a really, really good one?

Why Getting Rich In The Deep End Requires You to Own Your Market

Everything you want in your business comes from owning your market. Ownership brings respect, desirability, authority, process, systems, demand, scale, predictability, clarity, simplicity, and so much more.

Generalists thrive on the idea that anyone can be their client— and that each new client is a different set of problems to solve. The challenge, of course, is that this idea creates a lot of noise. Over the long run, that noise will leave you deaf. The generalist ends up attracting a lot of "bad fit" clients.

And the generalist has to spend a lot of time with every project and every client, learning a lot of things for the first time. Every new client becomes an exercise in re-inventing the wheel—an exhausting process that traps the business owner into being an operator for life.

Listen—I'm sure you are good at what you do. You probably have at least one expert-level skill. Maybe more, and you likely shy away from picking up new skills every week. After all, to master something, you need to focus more of your efforts on fewer skills. So why is this line of thinking somehow less critical when it comes to the market you serve?

How good will you ever be if, every month, you have to do a completely different line of work? One month you're a web developer; the next a web designer, then a search engine marketer, then a copywriter, public relations associate, email marketer, app developer, virtual assistant, growth hacker, and so on. If this were your approach, you'd be dead tired. Maybe even dead.

Yet agencies do this every day when it comes to the markets they serve. They work on a client project in a market, research the ins and outs of that market, start to get an idea of the problems they're experiencing, and then move to the next.

 **Generalizing your services is like sticking your toe in the shallow end of the pool: easy, safe, and limiting.**

Obviously, they're diving into waters that are only an inch deep. So they master that inch (if they don't break their neck first) and then go a mile wide to the next project for a client in a different market.

Their logic here is that they've learned the market for that one client and don't want to "get bored" working in it again. Plus, when each new client brings in a unique set of problems, each solution feels unique. (Forget for a second how much effort and energy was invested in decrypting those problems and building a solution.)

But I've worked with a lot of businesses that have successfully owned their market. So far, I've yet to meet one that is bored—or that feels like they're "solving the same problem every day."

When you own your market, what happens is a little more nuanced. Your energy and attention to problems shift to higher and higher-leveraged issues over time.

As a market owner, you'll see a pattern of problems within your market. You'll start to realize that each business coming to you for help has a few core issues that you can help solve. You'll build a solution for one client, but then you can re-use that solution for the next client and the next one.

Each time, the solution is just as valuable and exciting for the client, but yes, it will become more routine for you and your agency. Here's what will happen instead of boredom—after a few repetitions, you'll realize you can start to create systems.

 **Becoming a specialist allows you to confidently swim in the deep end with better customers and less competition.**

So instead of investing your energy in discovering new problems or building a unique solution, you'll create processes and methods to serve each subsequent client even better.

You'll spend your time improving the solution you have to make it incrementally better on every new project. And once you have systems in place to serve the customers in your market, you'll be able to identify seats in your business that can be delegated to part or full-time team members. Which, of course, will enable you to remove yourself as a full-time operator.

You'll create process playbooks and focus your energy on marketing your solution to the audience you serve. And for the first time, you'll start to see how you could scale your operation. In other words, you'll finally have a *business* and not just a well-paying *job*.

This evolution will continue to unfold until the challenges and problems you face start to look a lot more like vision and leadership problems.

How big can your enterprise grow? Or how small and lean and profitable can you engineer your systems to be? Could you systemize your business to the point that it could run without you? I don't know about you, but I feel like the problems of the market owner are anything but boring.

And if I had to guess, they are the types of things you *thought* you'd spend all your time working on as an entrepreneur.

What This Book Is Not

This book is all about how to get rich by focusing on your niche and owning your market, but I need to give you a warning first. The process I'm going to teach you in the following pages is not a *quick fix* for marketing, sales, or operations problems. You won't find the "magic key to growth" that you can implement in the next seventy-two hours to solve all of your issues.

However, the material in this book *can* have a profound impact on all areas of your business if you act on it. Indeed, the framework you're about to learn could *revolutionize* the market in which you intend to serve.

But this book is not a silver bullet. There is no one tactic here that will give you what you want. Some of my methods will feel counterintuitive. They might even cause short-term lulls in your business.

But as I mentioned earlier, *owning your market* is about you, not your market.

This book teaches you how to show up and present yourself in the market you want to serve. But markets are complicated things, and each will respond differently. We have no control over markets. At best, we can influence them—but even doing that requires you to *own your market* for a while.

What *do* we have complete control over?

Ourselves. And we control the content and context of the interactions we have in the marketplace. Naturally, then, this book will focus on what we *can* control: content, context, and interactions.

Every business owner starts from a different place. The journey to market ownership will be different for everyone. But one thing is certain: it *will* be a journey.

You might see unbelievable results in just a couple of short months. Or your journey could be longer—maybe a couple of years—and require a steadfast will to stay the course.

However, regardless of the time it takes to achieve your goal, I'm confident that what I'm about to teach you will transform your business—not just by helping you get more leads and revenue but by changing your mindset about how your business operates.

You should expect at least a few struggles along the way. Your journey will require you to overcome many challenges. You might find yourself:

- Turning down clients who don't fit your market focus.
- Disappointing current clients as you change direction.

- Accepting that the first market you chose to serve might not be the market you ultimately embrace.

- Dealing with rejection from publishers, associations, and strategic partners.

- Making a trade-off between working on revenue-generating projects now and working on your own business—without a return for weeks, months, or years.

While these are no doubt real and costly dilemmas, the good news is this: the upside to owning your market is unlimited.

There is no cap on the number of leads, customers, and revenue your business could generate within the market you choose to serve. Most markets can easily sustain several seven-figure agencies, while some can support even eight-figure businesses or more.

And once you finally do own your market—if you want to— you can usually expand your focus into broader or complementary spaces with speed and precision. I truly believe that owning your market is the key to providing yourself with the freedom you've always dreamed of.

And I hope, once you've finished this book, that you will too.

The Biggest Objection to Market Ownership

When talking with agency owners about niching and choosing a precisely defined market to pursue, without fail, the number one objection I hear is this:

"I can't imagine my clients would ever be okay with me working with their competitors."

Or some version of this. I even hear this when speaking to a room full of my own clients, all of which are digital agency owners who are paying me for the exact same service. The irony is not lost on me.

If you go down this path, you'll likely get as an objection from prospective clients—it's a very real issue. Your clients might perceive your work with others as a weakness or threat to their position in the market.

One of the stories I like to tell the most is of my own agency experience. When we focused on building websites and digital marketing solutions for restaurants in Denver, Colorado, we had about a dozen different clients with restaurants located on the same street. Four of these restaurants were next door to one another with different owners.

The very reason that these clients moved forward with us was *because* we worked with many businesses just like theirs. Instead of spending weeks or months having to learn their market, needs, and goals, we could quickly plug into their businesses to get them the results they so needed: more reservations and more walk-in diners.

 **Generalists say 'yes' to everything. Specialists say 'yes' when they can duplicate a past win.**

The more experience you have in your market, the more you are able to provide an experience that creates results for your clients. The drawbacks of working with a business that serves a specific market are far outweighed by the positives.

I think this objection can be resolved with a pretty simple question:

"Would you rather work with an agency with little to no experience working with businesses like yours? Or would you prefer to work with an agency that has worked with over one hundred businesses exactly like yours with proven processes, frameworks, and methodologies to get you the exact results you're looking for as fast as possible?"

So, when your prospective client raises this objection, put their mind at ease and let them know you never share client information with others, and that working with you is a clear advantage in the marketplace, not a threat.

One More Note About the Book

In this book, I might reference specific tactics, like publishing or speaking. However, the concepts you'll learn in these pages are well-suited to endless channels.

Yes, I'm just scratching the surface here—and that's out of necessity. There are plenty of experts who go deeper into a lot of the topics I hit in this book. My friend Pete Vargas can help you become a better speaker; my friend Re Perez can help you with branding and positioning. Russell Brunson can help you build crazy awesome funnels. Gary Vaynerchuk has resources to help you master social media and the entrepreneurial mindset. Nicholas Kusmich covers dominating with Facebook Ads. Brad Martineau teaches marketing automation. And Steven Pressfield can help you become a better writer. But my goal is to help you understand the fundamentals and how this stuff applies to your agency.

By the end, you'll be able to apply what I'm teaching to your business—and begin leveraging it to *own your market*. It's the equivalent of jumping feet first into the deep end of your niche.

Chapter One Take Aways for Getting Rich In The Deep End

◆ Being a renter or tourist in a market is when you just dip your toe in here and there. You don't proclaim that this niche is your people. You drop in, do some work, and move to the next. People that own their market jump in the deep end. They commit to staying out of the shallow end.

◆ Very few businesses end up owning their markets.

◆ When you tell people *exactly* who your ideal customer is, it gives them the opportunity to refer the right people to you.

◆ Make it easy for others to refer you by being clear on who your ideal customer is.

◆ Owning your market brings respect, desirability, authority, process, systems, demand, scale, predictability, clarity, simplicity, and so much more.

◆ Generalists thrive on the idea that anyone can be their client–they love having to solve new problems with every client they sign. This is reinventing the wheel.

◆ Specialists thrive on getting their clients a predictable result and doing a little better with each client. They hate reinventing the wheel. They just want it to go faster.

◆ Generalists say yes to everything. Specialists say yes when they've already gotten this exact result and can easily replicate it.

◆ Heart and brain surgeons make a lot more money than a general practitioner.

CHAPTER TWO

Heather Meets Her Mentor

Remember the story at the beginning of this book about Heather at the networking event? I know it well—because Heather told it to me.

Yes, if you haven't already guessed, that was my business card Jake handed her. She called me. Eventually. But I'll get to that soon enough. First, let me back up a bit.

When I met Heather Carlyle, she was like so many other agency owners. Her business was an unpredictable rollercoaster, and she survived on the goodwill of referrals and word of mouth.

And as you might expect, after running into Jake, having one project delayed, and watching another fall through, she was ready to make a change.

Heather told me before our first meeting that one night after her team went home, she sat down and ran some numbers. She realized that if she didn't get a new lead for her business fast, she'd not only have to downsize her team—but take a pay cut herself.

But both issues were problems Heather had faced before. So I asked her what was different about this time.

"I couldn't get Jake out of my head. There I was, struggling to figure out where my next client was going to come from, and he had a crowd of restaurant owners fighting for his attention. So I pulled your business card from my bag and started looking into what you did."

When Heather went to my website, she found boldly phrased invitations like these: "Create a predictable pipeline of clients." "Become a market authority." "Be the go-to professional in your market."

But even seeing Jake's success doing precisely these things, Heather admitted that she didn't think it was possible for her. Heather also confessed she was at her wits' end.

"I figured it couldn't hurt. So I thought, 'Why not?' I booked a session with you, and here we are. So how can I get more leads coming in like Jake? Is it about getting on stage at a couple of conferences? What's working right now for lead generation?"

I had to admit to Heather that I was no master of the ins and outs of the newest marketing tactics. I wasn't even aware that Jake had decided to make stages a part of his "own your market" strategy until Heather told me. But hearing that did bring a smile to my face—considering Jake had emphatically told me when we first met that he'd never do stages.

Heather went on.

"Marketing my clients' businesses is a big part of what I do. So I just don't understand why I'm having such a hard time doing it with my own. I've known for years that I'm supposed to pick a niche, but I just can't imagine building websites for doctors or dentists for the rest of my life. I don't see myself doing one thing over and over. I like solving new problems every day."

I told Heather that I've never seen a business owner do "just one thing" after working to own her market, but that I felt her apprehension about that. If I had to do only a single thing for the rest of my own life, I might get stir-crazy too.

 **Most business owners are "me-focused." They talk about what they do rather than the customer's problems. To scale successfully, transition to "customer-focused" language.**

Then I explained that she was facing a problem many professional services firms do. They find it easy to help their clients. After all, they're outside their clients' businesses and can look in with dispassion. But it's much harder for them to help themselves. As I often say, "It's hard to read the label on the bottle of wine when you're actually inside the bottle itself."

 **Generalists thrive on the idea that anyone's a client—they love solving new problems every time. They love treading water.**

Like many entrepreneurs, Heather hadn't yet developed the strategic thinking skills necessary to work on her own business. W. Edwards Deming, the father of business management, says, "A system cannot understand itself. Transformation requires a view from outside."[2]

Heather either needed me to help her or she needed to strengthen her ability to step outside of her business and treat herself as one of her own clients. Unfortunately, the second approach is hard to do—as we are often so emotionally, mentally, and financially vested in our own ventures.

I assured Heather that we would be working on her strategic thinking "muscle," helping her "zoom out" from working in her business so she could finally work on it. That would certainly help her solve the problem at hand. And, likely, many others that she had been ignoring for too long. But Heather was becoming visibly restless.

"Maybe you don't understand. This is an emergency. Will you be able to help me find leads, or what?"

With Heather's permission, I took her notebook and pen. At the top of a blank page, I wrote, "The 5 A's." Then down the page, I wrote five large capital A's. I handed Heather back the pen and book.

I said, "I'd like you to do a little exercise for me. We're going to fill in some things beside those A's.

"The first A stands for 'Audience.'

"Now, the most recent blog post on your website is titled, '5 Reasons Why Your Website Needs to be Responsive.' Who is the audience for that piece of content?"

Heather thought for a minute, then told me it was for businesses whose websites weren't responsive. After all, the post was literally five reasons why companies needed to move away from non-responsive sites.

I replied, "Okay, so for the first A on your page, write that down. As I explain each A, I'd like you to think about how it relates to both this single blog post and your broader strategy.

"The second A stands for 'Awareness.' How are you making this audience aware of you?"

It quickly became clear to me that Heather was like so many entrepreneurs I've worked with—she hadn't put much thought into why this particular blog post, or any other, was on her site.

She knew she "needed" to blog, so her team would occasionally add blog content to her website to make it look fresh and active. Heather told me that she guessed this audience would become aware by searching for "responsive web design" on search engines like Google—but that she actually had no idea if the page ranked for this term.

I thought for a moment. "Okay, so that's our awareness. Google—write that down.

"Now, in your blog post, you reference a client of yours. A business coach named Amy. And you show her project as a before-and-after example of what a responsive website project can do.

"I'm curious—is that how you found Amy? Did she Google 'responsive web design' or some other term to find you? Is responsive a word she knew before working with you? Because the third A stands for 'Attract.' Would this blog post attract people like Amy to inquire about working with you?"

Heather chuckled and replied with a sheepish grin.

"No, she wouldn't have known that term. Her focus is on being a business coach and growing her community of business coaches using her methods. It's definitely not on specific web design terms like responsive.

"I've known Amy since college. She came to me because she was frustrated that her website 'looked funny' on mobile phones. She was trying to grow her community of business coaches and was embarrassed by her site."

I nodded and moved on to the fourth A, Authority. I gently explained how Heather's blog post lacked a certain level of proof and credibility.

"You do have a before-and-after image, which is great. But you could be doing a better job to establish trust with your readers. We can come back to that, though. For now, write down 'before-and-after image' for 'Authority.'"

Then I asked what kind of results her website got for Amy's business.

Heather said, "Amy saw a massive uptick in the size of her email list. And she got a lot of new members for her virtual coaching community. Making her website and community mobile-friendly made a huge difference for her. And not only in terms of getting more clients. Now she can engage more with her community on the go, which means she isn't tied to her desk. That was really important to Amy."

These were awesome results, but her post lacked any mention of them. I asked why she didn't include these, and Amy replied, "I didn't want to brag."

I explained to Heather, as you can probably imagine yourself, those kinds of results would be desirable for a lot of other coaches, too.

But it was time to dive into the final A.

"Heather, the fifth A is how you intend to 'Acquire' the interest of what we typically regard as a lead."

"Sure, a visitor to your blog post could choose to voluntarily click the 'contact us' page on your website. However, you're not offering anything of value to give people a clear and compelling reason to contact you. Maybe that's a resource download, or a free consultation to assess the opportunity cost of having a website that's not mobile-friendly."

"There's no 'line of sight' here. In other words, we can't see a path to them becoming a customer unless they feel like contacting you."

"But that's okay for the purposes of this exercise, so write down 'contact us' as your fifth A."

Heather took a moment to look over her 5 A's. Then she sighed and said, "I don't think this blog post will help me find more people like Amy. That was what I really wanted, but I can see now that the approach seems half-baked."

Heather was making progress, so it was time to help her see the label from outside her bottle.

"Heather, I'd like you to look at your whole blog with this new lens. Take a look at the content on your website, too. How does it stand up when you think about the 5 A's?"

I slid my laptop over to her side of the table, with her website open in my browser. She dutifully clicked and scanned through page after page, but I could see that this new way of thinking was making Heather uncomfortable in her chair. After a few minutes, she slumped.

"I guess I'm not committed to a single audience. Everything is pretty generalized. It feels disconnected and messy. If I looked at it more closely, I'm sure I'd find that each blog post has a different set of 5 A's."

"*Haphazard* is the word that comes to mind. But I just can't see changing all of my website content to fix this problem. I don't have time! I need leads—like, yesterday! And in case it needs saying now, you're never going to get me to wear a chef hat like Jake either!"

I gave Heather another moment to think as she continued to scan her website. Then she looked back at her notebook with a sigh as if she were resigning herself to the shape her business was in. I wanted to make her feel better, but I had to tell her something important.

"Heather, what I'd like to have you do next is rethink your 5 A's with me right now. Then I'm going to ask you to invest in one small marketing activity using the 5 A's and your intuition as a guide.

"Owning your market means making conscious choices about your messaging, about the content you publish as a business. The 'wheres,' 'hows,' 'whys,' and 'whats' of the material you broadcast into the marketplace. And the way you react to your market's response to you.

"I'm not just talking about changing the headline on your website. I wish it were that easy! To own your market, you're going to need to go deeper than the cosmetic.

"You need to ask questions like this: Does this content help to establish me as an authority in the eyes of my reader? Was the message placed in a way to get maximum exposure for my business? Does it speak to the heart of my potential client's problems? Does it emanate trust and credibility? And do my lead capture, sales, and service delivery methods support this approach?

"Those are some big questions. But are you open to taking a look at all of this?"

Heather agreed, and over the next few minutes, we built a simple strategy using the 5 A's. Here is what it looked like:

Audience: business coaches

Awareness: Heather's friend Amy's own blog about being a business coach, Amy's email list, and her private Facebook group for coaches

Attract: how to launch an online course to make passive income, a guide specifically written for coaches

Authority: her stories and examples of doing this work for past clients

Acquire: a simple scheduler offering a sixty-minute "online course strategy building session"

With this basic strategy written down, I challenged Heather to one last task.

I told her to take out her phone and message her friend Amy to offer to create this "ultimate guide to building an online course for business coaches" as a guest post on Amy's blog. I gave Heather a simple script for her message, which she sent reluctantly.

 **Stop solving the same problem over and over again. Build systems that allow you to solve more fun problems in the future.**

"Amy is going to say no. I'm sure she already has other people creating content for her site and won't want anything from me. If she did, she would have asked me by now."

"Besides, I already told you—I can't see myself building websites and doing marketing for just business coaches."

I nodded, paused, and started to pack up my things.

"Heather, I appreciate you taking the time to meet with me today, but I don't have a silver-bullet solution for you.

"Working with me would be hard. You'd have to make big choices about where your business was headed and why you were doing what you were doing. And the 'Jake-level' results are far from guaranteed.

"At times, it would feel like you were taking three steps back for every step forward. So I understand—owning your market isn't for everyone, and it's okay if it's just not for you.

"If you change your mind, you know how to find me."

Understandably, Heather was shocked at my abrupt end to our meeting. But I shook her hand, thanked her for her time, and walked out of her office. In the parking lot, I was starting my car when Heather rushed up and knocked on my window.

"Amy got back to me. She said, 'Hell yeah' to the guide.

"What's next?"

Chapter Two Take Aways to Get Rich In The Deep End

◆ Niching isn't about solving the same problem over and over for the rest of your life. It's about building systems and solving more fun problems, like scaling your agency.

◆ You can't see the label from inside the bottle. You need a coach or mentor to help you understand the system that is your business from the outside.

◆ Clients don't buy your services, they buy a result. So, when you talk about your services, always put them in the context of the results you deliver.

◆ Don't build half-baked marketing strategies for your agency. Answer the 5A's with each activity: audience, awareness, attract, authority, and acquire.

◆ Owning your market is more than just updating the headline on your agency's website homepage.

◆ Choosing a niche is not a silver bullet. You have to work hard to build awareness, learn, and become masterful with everything that is your niche.

CHAPTER THREE

The 5-A Framework™

The internet tells us all the time that we need to be publishing content to grow our businesses. Some people call this "inbound" marketing or "content marketing." (Or even just "SEO" if the content is indexable by Google.)

But "content" is more than just articles or blogs on websites. It's at the heart of everything you do to communicate about your business.

Content is what's on your website's homepage. It's what your assistant says when he or she answers your phone. And it's how you introduce yourself at an event or on an elevator.

Even the name and tagline of your business is content. So content is king, right? Well, not quite. Gary Vaynerchuk, Master of Social Media, says, "Content is king, but context is god."[3]

Vaynerchuk means that it's not just about the content. You also have to consider the platform you are publishing to, the audience, the experience your content creates, and the consistency you deliver. This context—or, more precisely, the lack of it—is why I think most businesses get discouraged with marketing.

As entrepreneurs, we can no longer create random content and hope it gets results. The internet is organizing into hyper-focused, hyper-specialized niches, and the winners take all.

That means you need awareness about what you are trying to accomplish and who you serve. You need insight into where your customers are in their businesses—not where you are in yours—before you publish anything.

Most agency owners don't realize this—so their marketing is typically "me-focused." Most simply publish once in a while about what *they* are up to: a recent project launch, a technology they are interested in, or a reference to a trend or method they think is important.

And I've come to learn that when marketing is me-focused, the agency itself is very likely the same way. In other words, they either don't have a market or they're scared to communicate directly to their best clients because they might turn other ones away.

But that kind of me-focused myopia spreads out from marketing and leads to more significant business challenges. Specifically, it causes issues of scale. If you serve many different markets with just as many services, you'll eventually become unable to separate yourself from your business. You'll never be able to delegate things like marketing and sales—because only *you* will be aware of what type of work you're interested in taking on next.

And because you lack a clear understanding of your target market and their problems, you'll always struggle to determine what should be done *today* to drive leads. The alternative is creating a specialized, *customer-focused* business.

Customer-focused agencies spend a lot less time talking about themselves or their interests—and a lot more time speaking directly to their ideal customers. These agencies work to understand their perfect buyers and "get inside their heads," talking about their pains and problems and ideal outcomes and worldviews.

Most customer-focused agencies eventually go on to specialize, serving narrow, defined markets with only a couple of focused services that solve a small set of valuable problems.

And as a result, these agencies tend to earn more—not only because specialization helps them focus on fewer things but because it pushes them to become *better* at those things.

Why I Created the 5-A Framework

To help you become this kind of specialized, customer-focused agency, I have distilled my ideas and methods into the 5-A Framework. I created this simple framework for one reason—to help you get rich (and happy) by owning your market.

The 5-A Framework focuses on the same things I showed to Heather:

1. Audience

2. Awareness

3. Attract

4. Authority

5. Acquire

In this book, you'll find a chapter dedicated to each of these 5 A's. As you read, you'll achieve a greater understanding of how to implement each A into your business strategy. You'll also see relevant examples, as well as exercises to help you apply the ideas in your own business.

But before we move on, a note about the word *framework*. The choice was a deliberate one.

My method is about strategy and structure—and definitely *not* about following a formula. Use a formula, and you'd expect guaranteed results. Just put in X, and you'll get Y at the end. A framework, on the other hand, can yield very *different* results from one company to the next. For one business, inputting X could yield Y. For others, it could produce 1,000 Y.

It makes sense, then, that some agencies will learn this framework and invest the necessary time and resources to build a robust business. Others will dabble or resist certain aspects of owning their market—and will consequently struggle to get the same level of results.

In my experience, the 5-A Framework leads to market traction and success. Ignoring it creates more of what you're probably already experiencing: frustration and stagnation.

That's why I created the Framework and why I wrote this book: to help anyone put each of the 5 A's in place.

The 5 A's

Here, at a high level, are the 5 A's.

 **Audience. When you're clear on *who* your ideal client is, figuring out *where* to find them is easy.**

A1: Audience

Who are you speaking to? Answering that question lets you answer another, critical one: "Where do I find my ideal customer?" If your audience is always changing, the "where" will always change as well. That means your business will fail to build momentum.

Many businesses that don't have a well-defined audience leave a lot up to chance. They *hope* that, eventually, they'll attract people by going around and shouting about the problems they can solve.

This approach can sometimes work, but it usually leaves the agency struggling through feast-and-famine cycles, surviving on referrals and word of mouth.

Knowing who you're talking to, on the other hand, will give you clarity around many other key marketing questions. You'll know where you can look for your ideal customer, the types of problems they have, the characteristics they possess, how to leverage existing infrastructure to build authority, and so on.

Finally, knowing everything you can about your audience will also help you build the systems and processes that will help your business scale.

 **Awareness. Let people know about you by leveraging existing market infrastructure–don't reinvent the wheel or build your own audience.**

A2: Awareness

Now that you know who your audience is, how will you reach them? By doing some research and market validation, you can start creating lists of opportunities to build awareness for your business.

This will involve at least one channel—a path to customers in your market—and maybe more. You'll also define a set of repetitive activities to reach those channels.

What does a channel look like? It can be an industry blog that gets lots of traffic. A targeted audience on the Facebook Ads platform. A strategic partner who already sells to a large group of your ideal customers. An in-person event, and so on.

And just as you focus your efforts on a narrow market by defining your audience, you'll also work to find one or two winning awareness channels. By zeroing in on just a couple, you'll have an easier time making your market aware of who you are, the problems you solve, and how you can add value to their business or organization.

 **Attract. Whisper the right things in the right places. Always talk about what you do in the context of your clients' biggest challenges and desired outcomes.**

A3: Attract

What costly problems or valuable opportunities—as the customer understands them—can you speak to? And can you speak about those problems and opportunities in *their* language? Because although you're an expert at the skills and services your business provides, your client is not.

I call this "the expert-to-client gap." To be successful, you need to meet your customers "where they are" and then close that gap.

Here's what your prospective clients *are* experts on—their own pain. They're more than familiar with their own struggles, their own businesses, and the situations they find themselves in.

To get the most attention in your market, you must be ready and willing to set your own expertise aside and speak directly to their struggle. The more fluent you are in the language and worldview of your ideal customer, the more you will attract.

This will feel counterintuitive. You'll spend more time speaking about what your customers do than you ever wanted to.

But you'll also be educating your prospective clients on the fact that problems they're experiencing are mere symptoms of deeper issues in their businesses. (Deeper issues, of course, that can be solved by your services.)

 **Authority. You need to crown yourself as an authority in your market. No one is going to do that for you. Tell people exactly why they should listen to what you say.**

A4: Authority

Are you building trust and credibility? If you create more authority in your market before a prospective customer contacts your business, your sales process will move faster, and your client will be more willing to do what you tell them. It's that simple.

Authority is the greatest accelerant in marketing. If working to own your market is like starting a fire, authority is lighter fluid.

So how do you build authority? In two ways: by getting other people in your market to talk about you, and by showing your prospective clients that you get results.

I've seen the power of both of these activities, and I've watched them help many agency owners become "go-to experts" in their markets in just a few short months.

Humans are, after all, social creatures, and we look to others around us to help us understand who to trust. When we see that people we respect have come to trust someone, it is almost impossible to avoid trusting them ourselves.

It's the same with social proof like testimonials and case studies. They carry a lot of weight with people who are looking for reassurance about solving their problems with you.

That means that the more influential your third-party endorsements are—and the more proof you can show that you solve problems within your market—the more sales-ready your prospective clients will be when they come to you.

 **Acquire. Sales for agencies happen in conversations. Every marketing activity must have a clear path to a conversation.**

A5: Acquire

How are you converting interested visitors to leads? Too many businesses leave this part up to chance. They simply put a "contact us" button in their navigation and hope that interest will manifest into viable leads on the first point of contact.

This is a problem—because at *no* point in your marketing activities and systems should you be leaving your strategy up to hope.

But I'll show you how to make it incredibly simple for your ideal customer to engage with your company or express their interest in having you follow up with them over time.

And when you're done, each of your awareness activities will either help you get an appointment scheduled or add an email address to your list of prospective clients.

The Power of the 5 A's

By implementing even just one of the 5 A's into your strategy, you'll be better off than if you hadn't put any in place.

For instance, let's say all you do is build *authority* for your business by getting third-party endorsements and showing proof of results. You'll find you speed up the process of building trust and credibility with new prospective customers.

But like the Greek philosopher Aristotle theorized, the whole is greater than the sum of its parts.[4] While each of the 5 A's will add value to your business, together they'll work for even greater gains.

The 5-A Framework can transform your business—taking it from one that's reliant on the whims of referrals and word of mouth to a growth machine.

When you implement all the pieces of the 5-A Framework, you'll go from being a market tourist to a market owner and experience a whole new way of being an entrepreneur. I promise you'll even *feel* different.

Based on what I've seen happen when agencies implement my framework, here's what you can expect:

- Increased traffic and inbound leads from 5-A content
- More educated "raving fans" who are ready to buy because of the authority you've built
- More and better clients
- Higher prices (owing to your status as an expert in your market)
- More business with existing clients that re-engage from your content (instead of just forgetting you when their project is over)
- More strategic partnerships with others who serve the same market you do
- Better access to connectors in your market (because influencers like to be friends with other influencers)
- More contacts, fans, followers, and evangelists
- Increased interactions with people in your audience (and shorter sales cycles as a result)
- More demand for you, the expert in your market
- Greater ease creating productized services, because you have better insight into the persistent problems that people in your market face

- Higher profit margins (because you're either charging more or working less)

Many agencies already using the 5-A Framework have also told me about other benefits beyond what I could have imagined. They have shown me how owning their market has helped them achieve freedom in their business and life. They've reported they now feel they have a *business* and not just a job for themselves.

I am confident that by implementing this framework, you'll achieve some or all of the benefits I've listed here, as well as others that might surprise you.

Do me a favor. As you implement what you learn while reading, please let me know more about your journey in our private Facebook group: OwnYourMarket.com/fb.

How to Use the 5-A Framework

Tactics and technologies change, but the high-level concepts I discuss in this book have been relevant for the entire twenty years I've been an entrepreneur.

Yes, it's possible that specific platforms or tactics I mention in this book might operate differently in the future. But the core ideas and strategies are universal, and they'll apply to any channel.

The same goes for markets. The 5-A Framework can be applied no matter what kind of audience you're trying to reach. Each market will have its nuances, but remember—markets exist because numerous people have problems they're trying to solve or opportunities they're pursuing. Find a way to get in touch with one of those groups and offer specific help for a defined problem, and you'll succeed.

Here's a caution, however, in case you didn't infer as much from Heather's story. Yes, I'm confident that the 5-A Framework and the concepts taught in this book will get results. However, those results will vary greatly. In particular, it's not realistic to expect immediate, instant, business-changing results from a few hours of work.

While you might experience some quick *wins*—and you might even get massive traction—this book is not a quick *fix* for your business. Owning your market is a process that requires commitment and sustained action over time.

Your own journey will probably be like solving a complex puzzle. You'll need to decode deep-rooted psychological needs and desires within large populations of businesses and organizations.

You'll be analyzing patterns and connecting the decentralized web of complexity that exists in your market. Not exactly "done in an afternoon" stuff.

Finally, one more note. I know that what I'll teach you will change the way you think of your business. But there's also a high probability that applying the principles in this book will change *you* as a person.

Following the methods in this book might indirectly lead you to core questions about *why* you do the work you do. You might wonder about *what* you really enjoy doing, or *how* you want to operate your business from day to day. These questions might feel uncomfortable at first, but you'll be fine, and they'll certainly be worth it.

Some clients I've worked with were very close to owning their market when we first started working together. They made a couple of small tweaks to their strategy and implementation and their business shot off like a rocket ship.

Other clients went through a complete makeover. They ended up changing their company name, redefining their service offering, restructuring their team, and overhauling all of their business processes to meet the needs of their market.

But through it all, I watched them do the work and make the hard decisions to build a better business. I saw them face challenge after challenge with optimism and a steadfast desire to achieve freedom in their business and life.

And I worked beside them as they experienced great joy—as did I—when they emerged from this tunnel of transformation. But I can't tell you what kind of client you'll be. You—and you alone—have control over how you want this journey to play out.

The work is worth it—but don't pretend for a second that there won't be work. Find joy in the process, learn as much as you can, and have some fun along the way.

Chapter Three Take Aways to Get Rich In The Deep End

━━━━━━━━━

- Content is at the heart of everything you do to communicate about your business. From your business name, homepage headline, to a Facebook video. What you say at every touchpoint matters.

- Most agency owners' websites are "me-focused." They talk about the agency, their projects, their services—to own your market you need to transition your language to "customer-focused" language. Talk about their problems more than what you do.

- Audience

- When you're clear on *who* your ideal client is, figuring out *where* to find them is easy.

- Awareness

- Let people know about you by leveraging existing market infrastructure—don't reinvent the wheel or build your own audience—stand on the shoulders of giants.

- Attract

- Whisper the right things in the right places. Always talk about what you do in the context of your clients' biggest challenges and desired outcomes.

- ◆ Authority
- ◆ You need to crown yourself as an authority in your market. No one is going to do that for you. Tell people exactly why they should listen to what you say.
- ◆ Acquire
- ◆ Sales for agencies happen in conversations. Always make sure you have a clear path from awareness to you having a call with an ideal prospect.
- ◆ Results don't come from choosing a niche and doing a few hours of work. You need a sustained commitment to succeed in your niche over time.

CHAPTER FOUR

Heather Chooses Her Audience

A couple of weeks later, in the corner of a busy little café near the EMA office, Heather walked in to meet me. When she sat down with her latte, I could tell right away she seemed less than happy. I was about to ask if the "Ultimate Guide" post she was writing for Amy fell through, but she cut me off.

"So yeah, the whole 'pick an audience' thing backfired."

I couldn't tell whether she was just being confrontational or whether she was actually upset.

"I need to find another niche."

I asked her to take a step back and explain. Turns out Amy did publish the guide on her blog. And, even better, Amy invited Heather into her private Facebook Group to answer questions and engage with her members as a guest expert.

"Things went great at first," Heather said.

I raised an eyebrow, curious about what had happened to take the shine off things, but she didn't notice.

"I got a bunch of new followers on social media, and this one coach even emailed me to set up a call. She wants to talk about building an online course.

"Amy asked for another article, too. She wants me to pitch her on some new article ideas."

Finally, I was too confused to stay quiet. "Heather, I don't understand why you think you need to find another niche. All of this sounds great! What's up?"

"Well," Heather replied, "I guess I feel like I said everything there is to be said about launching an online course in my guide. I don't really know what else I could write for Amy.

"And to tell you the truth, I'm kind of skeptical about that lead. It's not really normal to get a response like that so quickly, is it? They're probably just a tire-kicker, trying to find out whether or not they can even afford EMA."

I cocked my head. "Those seem like—well, they seem like small problems, to be honest. Is there something else?"

Heather sighed.

"Yes. Someone commented on my article about wanting help launching their own course."

I was still waiting for the other shoe to drop. "And..."

Heather flushed. "And then someone responded that this company, Course Launch, was a great company and they should contact them instead of me!"

I connected the dots—Heather was experiencing what I call a "someone stole my idea!" moment.

I could almost taste the doubt and fear seeping into the café around us. I tried to put into context all the positive results Heather had captured with just a single guest post. New followers. An active conversation within a private social media group. And an actual lead! All with a guide that she hadn't wanted to write in the first place.

 ## Proof of competition means there's a market for what you're offering.

But I could tell that my words were falling on deaf ears, so I tried to address the competitor issue.

"Heather, I promise you that within a week, you won't think of Course Launch as a threat to your business, but an asset.

"You're considering it a bad thing, but finding a competitor in your target market is actually great. Competitors are proof that a market exists for what you're trying to sell! I'd much rather see any of my clients competing with other companies than trying to create something unproven.

"But for now, I don't want to get distracted by Course Launch. I'd like to focus on two other issues today, which I think are the core of what you're saying. You want to know whether this market is right for you in the long run. And you want to know how to come up with new article ideas to pitch Amy."

Heather agreed. Over the rest of our meeting, I walked Heather through a couple of core tools to help with her audience strategy.

The first was what I call a MarketMap™—a short document meant to collect the names of publishers, strategic partners, associations, conferences, and, yes, even competitors in Heather's chosen market.

The second tool I showed Heather was a "customer avatar" profile—a description of a fictional person that best represented a combination of her ideal customers and their demographic, geographic, and psychographic traits. (You'll learn more about both of these tools in the next chapter.)

I also gave Heather the exercises and examples outlined in *Own Your Own Market*. And I asked her to complete several assignments for the next time we met.

1. Complete her MarketMap.

2. Create a customer avatar for an ideal client in her market.

3. Brainstorm twenty headline ideas for new articles.

4. Call her competitor, Course Launch, and introduce herself.

Heather was dumbfounded. With the help of the Field Guide, she figured she could get through the MarketMap and the avatar, but she balked at the other two pieces of homework.

"Twenty headlines? I can't come up with three! And why on earth would I call my competitor?"

I stressed that it would all make sense soon and set a new date for a meeting. I was somewhat worried when she left, but, thankfully, Heather had always been the type of entrepreneur who enjoyed following instructions, and would take action even if she wasn't sure of the results she might get.

So I was reasonably confident that if I gave her work to do, she'd eventually get down to business and do it. Sure enough, Heather started doing her homework as soon as she got back to the office.

When we met about ten days later, she started by showing me her MarketMap (Exhibit 2).

Exhibit 2

MARKET MAP™				
Publishers	Partners	Events	Complimentary	Competitors
Amy's Blog	International Coach Federation	Coaching Now	Camilo PR	Course Launch
Action Coach	Assoc. of Corporation Executive Coaches	Million Dollar Coach	Fawn Advertising	Coach Website 365
The Business Coach Blog	Intl. Authority for Prof. Coaching	Prestige Coaching	WILDSTORY	BizCoach Marketing Inc.
Passion for Business	Amy	Get Attitude	Advance Your Reach	EasyWeb123
EMyth Blog		Events	Influencer Hub	
Center for Executive Coaching				

The MarketMap showed some publishers in the space, a couple of organizations selling in the same market that Heather could partner with—and yes, Amy was one of them. Heather had also listed the International Coach Federation, the Association of Corporate Executive Coaches, and the International Authority for Professional Coaching & Mentoring. There were also several conferences on her MarketMap, and, yes, even a few more competitors.

She had also created a customer avatar for a coach named Chris. While Chris wasn't a real person, Heather had drawn what she "knew" about him from conversations she'd had with real people in her audience. The traits she had extracted from these interviews helped her construct a character, give him a name, and bring him to life.

Now, instead of creating content aimed at a generic audience, she could speak specifically to Chris—someone who was struggling with the "time for money" grind that many coaches face, and who was short on the time he needed to spend to push into six figures of revenue.

 **Never just talk about services. Always talk about what you'll deliver in the context of outcomes. Clients buy results.**

Heather now understood that her ideal customer needed to figure out how to start leveraging his time better—so he could finally have the energy to invest in both his business and his family.

And that kind of clarity around her customer's challenges paid off immediately—Heather had had a much easier time brainstorming article headlines. In fact, she created not just twenty but twenty-one:

1. "7 Steps Coaches Can Use to Leverage Their Time with Online Courses"

2. "The Simple Guide to Creating an Online Course for Coaches"

3. "Why an Online Course Can Help You Overcome the Time for Money Problem"

4. "Coaches! Break the Six Figure Barrier with an Online Course"

5. "3 Mistakes Every Coach Makes When Launching an Online Course"

6. How to Make Passive Income As a Business Coach

7. "Critical Steps to Overcome 'Time for Money' in Your Coaching Business"

8. "11 Tools to Launch Your Online Course"

9. "Typical Upfront Costs When Launching an Online Course"

10. "How to Make Six Figures—Even Seven Figures!—with an Online Course"

11. "How to Leverage an Online Course in Your Coaching Practice"

12. "Why Online Courses Help Coaches Become Better at Coaching"

13. "7 Reasons Your Clients Need a Course That Supplements Your Coaching"

14. "Should You Sell Your Course for Monthly Fee or Charge Clients Once?"

15. "How to Build Your Course As a Membership Website"

16. "Can Your Course Drive Recurring Revenue for Your Coaching Practice?"

17. "How to Turn Your Coaching Process into a Repeatable System"

18. "Why Making Money While You Sleep Isn't a Myth"

19. "3 Things You MUST DO When You Plan Your Online Course"

20. "Optimizing Your Online Course: The 3 Tools You Need"

21. "How to Choose the Right Online Platform for Your Coaching Course"

Looking at that list, Heather couldn't help but wonder what would happen if Amy—or other publishers in her market—said yes to all of these articles.

Sure, she'd have to invest a good deal of time writing them, but after she'd gotten such good results from the "Ultimate Guide" on Amy's site, the possibilities were really starting to excite her.

Heather had finally realized that if she followed through on this work, she would easily be seen as an expert in helping business coaches launch courses online—and feel like one herself.

Therefore, after procrastinating and making excuses, and "coincidentally" always needing to do something else, Heather finally reached out to Course Launch, too.

Chapter Four Take Aways to Get Rich In The Deep End

◆ Finding others like you targeting your niche is a *good thing*, not a bad thing. Proof of competition means there's a market. It's a lot easier to sell to people who already believe in what you do than trying to convert non-believers.

◆ It's a lot harder to sell religion to non-believers than it is to get the religious to change denominations.

◆ People you think are your competitors probably are more valuable as friendly strategic partners than sworn enemies.

◆ Mapping your market allows you to find existing infrastructure. Stand on the shoulders of giants.

◆ When you speak to everyone, you speak to no one. When you're writing content for your market, write to one ideal person and you'll attract everyone in a market that connects with them.

CHAPTER FIVE

The First A—Audience

You're likely familiar with being part of an audience. Maybe you've sat in the crowd at a concert, or gone to a conference, or heard a sermon. But when you read this book, I want you to forget what it feels like when you're "out there."

Instead, visualize the other view at a big event—the one where you're looking *from* the stage at the many people in front of you. Think of them patiently waiting to get some value: entertainment, inspiration, motivation, knowledge, or experience.

That's *your* audience—the first A in the 5-A Framework—and they're ready for you.

How to Think About Your Audience

Not every audience is helpfully collected in a single auditorium for you to speak to. Today, thanks to the internet in general—and social media in particular—most audiences are loosely gathered in online networks of contacts, influencers, publishers, and connectors. In order to identify our market and know where to look for our ideal clients, we must be abundantly clear about who they are. But for our purposes, *where* they are matters less right now. It matters more simply *who* they are.

And to get down to finding out who they are and figuring out what they look like, let's split our market up into four different levels. Each is related to your audience as a whole:

- Primary Audience
- Secondary Audience(s)
- Customer Segment
- Ideal Customer

 It's a lot harder to sell religion to non-believers than it is to get the religious to change denominations.

Your Primary Audience

Your primary audience is a broad group of people. (Or it should be, anyway.) This is your main market—or niche—that you want to serve. This market should be made up of thousands of prospective clients.

You don't define who they are, nor should you. Your primary audience already exists—and all you're doing when you identify one is acknowledging that it's partly made up of the people you want to sell to. At some level, a primary audience must self-identify as you're thinking about them. If you tell people that you work with this market, they should easily be able to know whether or not they belong or know someone that does (so they can refer you, of course).

Here's an example: Colorado lawyers. You may not want to sell to *all* Colorado lawyers. You might, in fact, only want to approach a small subset of that audience.

Regardless, by identifying your *primary* audience, you'll be able to identify several specific awareness channels you can use to reach them. (More on this in Chapter 7.)

Your Secondary Audience(s)

Secondary audiences are usually larger groups of people that contain a subset of your primary audience. You can't define them either—like your primary audience, secondary audiences already exist whether you want them to or not.

What's a secondary audience? Here's an example. If your primary audience is Colorado lawyers, "business attorneys in the United States" might be a secondary audience. Some percentage of all US business attorneys' practice in the state of Colorado.

Not *all* business attorneys in the US are Colorado lawyers, obviously, and not all Colorado lawyers are business attorneys, but by speaking to US business attorneys, you'll be able to target a certain number of Colorado lawyers. Bingo: "business attorneys in the US" is a secondary audience.

Secondary audiences are important because you'll likely find that your market won't be organized into one neat group you can target. Maybe your primary audience is too small, and you need to look more broadly. Or perhaps your primary audience is actually made up of several broader secondary audiences.

Either way, identifying secondary audiences is an important part of marketing to the people you want to reach.

Interestingly, as you seek publishers, influencers, and trade groups, you'll often find that they're a secondary audience. In other words, some percentage of their own following is made up of people you want to reach. File this away for later because I'll come back to it.

Your Customer Segment

Your customer segment is the spectrum of ideal buyers within your primary audience and secondary audiences. A customer segment is a "target." That means the further away from your segment you get, the less of a fit a prospect will be for your business.

And unlike your primary and secondary audiences, you *do* get to define your customer segment—usually by a combination of demographic, geographic, and psychographic constraints. For example, law firms with over $1 million in annual billings based in Colorado that are frustrated with their website.

Your Ideal Customer

Once you have a grip on what your customer segment looks like, then it's time to zero in on an individual in that segment. This is your "ideal customer."

I highly recommend you identify one. Because when you're creating content and messaging for your business, speaking to "everyone" is a bad strategy. If you try to talk to everyone, you'll wind up talking to no one.

However, it can be difficult to remind yourself to talk to a single individual. That's why I recommend using a tool called a "customer avatar" to help create a fictitious example of our ideal customer.

By thinking of this "person" who has real qualities that you can humanize, a customer avatar can help you get much more specific in your messaging and marketing.

Here's an example: John is a business attorney who lives in Wash Park in Denver, CO. He's married with two kids and enjoys waking up early so he can get a run in before heading into his law practice for the day. He just became an associate partner. He's looking for new ways to help his practice grow to make more money and impress the more senior partners.

Your ideal customer is a Colorado lawyer who works at a firm that does at least $1 million in billings. But when you think of him as "John," your marketing becomes much more human. It's easier to write to John than it is to "Colorado lawyers," isn't it?

If you want help creating your customer avatar, download your *free* Get Rich In The Deep End Field Guide at ownyourmarket.com/guide.

How to Identify Your Audience

There's no magic formula to settling on which audience to target. I often get asked about whether I think selling to a specific market makes sense, and the truth is I *wish* I had this type of crystal ball. I could make *A LOT* of money if I did.

No, determining what market to go after is a decision that *you* need to make. I can't give you the right answer about choosing your audience, or even promise that you won't change your mind later once you finally choose one. (I've yet to meet one entrepreneur that fell in love with the first audience they identified and stopped there.)

What I am certain of is this: it's more important to *make a decision* and start working the 5-A Framework than it is to sit in inaction.

More than knowing who you serve, identifying an audience gives you clarity and direction when you wake up in the morning. And that clarity will help you invest with precision in marketing activities that put you in front of your ideal customers. So how do you identify a good one?

Choosing a Good Customer Segment

As you think about which customer segment to target, ask yourself these eleven questions:

1. Can you reach this customer segment easily through existing 'market infrastructure' like blogs, podcasts, associations, and events?

2. Does your target segment have compelling problems, opportunities, or needs?

3. Do decision-makers in the segment have money to spend?

4. Are decision-makers *willing* to spend money to solve their problems?

5. Are there enough potential sales in your segment to support your business over time? (In other words, is the segment large enough?)

6. Is your target market so large that you can't effectively communicate with them? You want them to see your message multiple times.

7. Can you compete to win customers?

8. Is there *too much* competition?

9. Can you own your market in the segment?

10. Do you *want to* own your market in the segment?

11. Can you develop repeat business?

Answering these questions will help you decide whether the customer segment you're considering is a good fit. But if that's too much for you, Exhibit 3 is a simple visual way to think about all of these criteria:

Exhibit 3

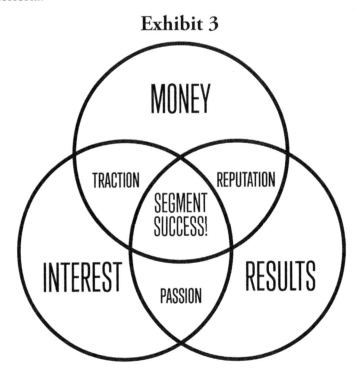

This model asks three questions:

- Where is the *money?*
- What captures your *interest?*
- And what kind of *results* can you demonstrate?

Let me explain a little further.

Money. Does your customer segment have money? More importantly, are you going to go after it?

In any customer segment, there are the top 20% who produce 80% of the results. Then you have the mushy middle 60%—and then there's the bottom 20%. They all make a commensurate amount of money—the top 20% making the most and the bottom 20% making the least.

But when people choose a customer segment, they often focus on that bottom 20%. Maybe that's because it feels safer or because they're simply not confident in their choice. Whatever the reason, they charge ahead and pursue customers that aren't making any money.

And then, for some reason, they get confused when those customers don't buy their services or don't have big budgets. Here's why: typically, clients spend about 7% of their annual revenue on marketing, advertising, and digital marketing services.

If you're trying to sell to an audience that only makes $100,000 per year in revenue, they probably only have about $7,000 bucks to spend—not just on *your* services, but on *everything* that looks and smells like marketing. Not great candidates for your $25,000 solution—or even your $10,000 one.

A $1 million business, on the other hand, typically spends $70,000 or more on marketing every year. If you're pitching $25,000 websites with a retainer on the back end—all of a sudden, that's actually possible for them to buy.

Interest. It's not enough simply to know that your client can afford what you do. You need to be interested in the work as well.

Notice I didn't say "passionate." Passion is something that can grow when you're interested in your work and you're getting results for your clients. You don't need to be passionate about what you do right away, or even at all. I'm passionate about road biking, but I'm probably not going to build a business based on it.

But do you have an interest in this segment? Are there things about it that seem interesting to you? Because when you're on the outside of a segment, you really don't know anything about it. So, at first, you'll need to be interested in diving in and finding out what you need to know.

Results Can you get results for this segment? And will you be able to demonstrate them? If you're looking at a customer segment but you really can't provide them any kind of results—or nobody wants or needs the results you can provide—then that's a big problem.

Reputation, Traction, and Passion

Now take a look at where those circles intersect.

When businesses have money, and they're willing to spend that money on the results you can get, you'll grow your reputation. The better your reputation, the more clients you'll attract—and the more money you'll make.

Then, when you're making money doing something that interests you, you'll have the stamina and the drive it will take to start getting traction in a segment. The more traction you get, the more interest you'll get, and so on. Traction and interest are self-sustaining.

And finally, when you're interested in something that gets great results, time and again, for clients—*that's* where passion comes from. It happens naturally, as an outgrowth of pride in your work.

And that passion will inspire you to put in more effort to get better and better results. This will fuel your passion, which will lead to more effort, and so on. It's the best kind of virtuous cycle.

Now put them all together—reputation, traction, and passion—and what do you have? True success in a customer segment.

Looking for Market Infrastructure

Hold on, though. Before you go charging into a customer segment, there's one more factor that should weigh into whether it's a good fit. Every good audience has existing "market infrastructure" you can tap into—events, publishers, associations, influencers, complementary businesses, and competitors.

You want to pay attention to that infrastructure because your customer segment is going to end up finding out about you in one of two ways: either through referrals and word of mouth, or because of whatever marketing and sales techniques you're using to reach out to them.

Yes, referrals and word of mouth are great, but building your own audience from scratch so you can market and sell to them is a time-consuming proposition. Why reinvent the wheel? Instead, look to the infrastructure in your market.

Malcolm Gladwell, the author of *The Tipping Point* and other books, popularized the idea that every audience has "connectors" and "super-connectors."[5] These are generous social butterflies who freely connect their friends and colleagues with others who can help them.

When you find these connectors and super-connectors, you can simply "snap in" to their existing audience and leverage the power of the work they've done before you—instead of painfully building your own audience over many months or years.

Tapping into someone else's audience can help your business get into the fast lane and help you overcome the "feast or famine" cycle that often accompanies referrals and word of mouth.

And that's where market infrastructure comes in. When you deliberately connect with your audience *where they are,* you can more easily build a pipeline of interest, an email list, and fans.

For example, if I were looking to get access to lawyers in my market, I could pay a relatively small fee to attend an event or conference put on by my state's Bar Association. This small investment could put me in the room with hundreds—or even thousands—of my ideal customers.

Compare that to the decades it has taken those Bar Associations to establish themselves as authorities in their markets. I imagine they've spent millions of dollars and countless hours building up lists of lawyers and convincing those lawyers to attend events. And all you have to do is pay a small registration fee and you can get in front of them!

Being able to leverage this kind of *market infrastructure* for your business is crucial to success in a customer segment. So, ideally, you should be able to do an hour or two of online research and easily find "proof of life" within the segment you're considering:

- Publishers
- Associations
- Blogs
- Podcasts
- Influencers
- Coaches
- Consultants
- Software providers
- Complimentary service providers
- Competitors
- Events and conferences

You might not find *all* of these easily, but you should be able to find at least *some* of them in order to green-light a customer segment.

If you can't, perhaps you're thinking about your segment differently than it organizes itself. Back to the drawing board.

Organizing What You Find

I often see people reach out to only a single organization or market influencer to get exposure in a new market, but doing so puts all of their eggs in one basket. That's a significant barrier to success. For example, let's say you're trying to get exposure on a podcast in your market. If you only reach out to a single podcaster, then a lot is riding on that interaction.

Perhaps it takes that podcast host weeks to get back to you. Maybe they end up turning you down. That's a lot of misspent effort. Worse, sitting around wastes an awful amount of time.

On the other hand, let's say you have a list of twenty podcasts, and you reach out to all of them in one sitting. One of the twenty gets back to you with an urgent deadline for setting up an interview because they had a guest cancel on them and your inquiry was just in time. That means the other *nineteen* can say no and you've still gotten results.

That's why I always recommend that my clients identify and pursue multiple opportunities. Keeping track of those opportunities can be a hassle, though, so I created a tool I call the MarketMap, which leverages the power of a list to get results. (In fact, I sometimes call it a list on steroids.) And because it's list-based, it does three critical things for you.

First, it helps you organize your market infrastructure in a single place. Second, it enables you to leverage the power of lists to get results for your business.

Third—and most importantly—it keeps you motivated. Because it's highly likely that when you reach out to people in your newly chosen market, you won't get results. The people you contact won't get back to you, or they'll say you're not a fit for what they do, or give you some other version of "no."

Letdowns like that can quickly become frustrating and demoralizing—unless you can look at a list full of other opportunities that might say yes.

Capture the information about your market infrastructure on your MarketMap, just like you saw Heather do in the last chapter. If you'd like help creating one, download the Get Rich In The Deep End Field Guide at ownyourmarket.com/guide.

Avoiding "Analysis Paralysis"

As I mentioned earlier, the most important thing to do at this point is to *make a choice*. I know firsthand that this can be a stressful decision, and the factors in play can become paralyzing.

After all, not only will you have to choose a market, but you'll have to consider the problems and solutions you'll focus on within that market. You'll also have to figure out *how* to talk about those problems because that may also influence your ability to reach your desired audience.

This stress is part of the reason I've tried out more than a dozen different audiences in my business life:

1. Self-employed artists
2. Denver nightclubs
3. Denver small businesses
4. Nonprofits based in Colorado
5. Colorado independent restaurants
6. Adobe Business Catalyst partners (a subset of web designers)
7. Medical marijuana dispensaries (I live in Colorado—I had to try!)
8. Educational consultants
9. Reconstructive dental surgeons
10. Peer-to-peer lenders
11. Web designers
12. Web professionals
13. Digital agencies

Lucky thirteen? I certainly think so.

Here's what you can learn from my thirteen-segment journey—when it feels like things aren't working out, it's okay to try something new and keep going.

I see many agency owners become paralyzed when they're trying to pick the right market—so much so that they never jump into the water. I would much rather see a client go *all-in* with a market for six or twelve months and work the 5-A Framework relentlessly only to find out that a segment isn't right for them. That's so much better than watching them spend the same time stuck in indecision.

My mentor, Craig Ballantyne, reminds me to take action when I lack clarity.

Working the steps in the remainder of the book on *any* market will have a materially positive effect on the work you do—with the added benefit of changing your mindset about what's possible with your business. That is a great value—one that should be recognized and pursued.

 **When you speak to everyone, you speak to no one.**

Creating a Customer Avatar

Having a customer segment still isn't enough—you need to dive deeper and get to know who your ideal customer is. And you do that with a customer avatar.

A customer avatar is really just a composite character that represents one ideal customer. You create it out of traits that your customers have in common.

Creating one will help you understand what motivates your customers to buy. And referring to one when you make marketing decisions will help you push through a lot of tricky spots.

When you're writing, recording, or speaking to communicate about your business and build authority in your market, everything else gets a lot easier when you talk to your customer avatar. People in the audiences I serve at UGURUS often tell me things like:

"Brent, your emails were in my head!"

"That blog post you wrote was exactly what I'm struggling with!"

"I told my husband I think you might be spying on me!"

That last one is no joke. A longtime customer thought I was reading her emails and chat messages because what I was writing was so close to the struggles and pains she endured every day.

Being that "dialed in" is no accident. I try hard to show I understand my customers' pains. While I do have a lot of experience as a digital agency owner, much of what I know comes from speaking with customers in the audience I serve—and then creating avatars based on what I hear. To start thinking about your customer avatar, ask yourself these kinds of questions:

- What does your ideal customer's morning routine look like?

- How does their business interact with their personal relationships?

- What are they thinking as their head hits the pillow at night?

Then dive deeper into the following categories.

Demographics

Your customer segment will already provide you with a broad range of demographic constraints. For example, over $1 million in revenue, operating in Colorado, and so on.

But you need to narrow that down to a single business operating in this market. Since we are creating an avatar or *fictional person*, you can make up whatever you want. (If you can base this on a real person you've served in the market, that makes this exercise relatively easy.)

- What's their name?
- How much money do they make in a year?
- How many employees or partners do they have?
- Where do they work?
- What does their family life look like?

Those answers could look like this:

- Architect named Jill
  - Runs a $2.5 million/year firm
  - Three partners plus a team of ten associates and admins
  - Downtown Denver office in LoDo; in a historic building
  - Married with two children
  - 42 years old

As you can imagine, speaking to everyone in your customer segment would force you into broad generalities. You would struggle to talk about the impact you could have on the problems in their lives.

However, by answering these questions, you'll have "a person" that you can imagine—Jill—with specific problems.

Psychographics

Make no mistake—knowing customer demographics will bring value to your customer avatar.

However, for me, the real value lies in psychographics: the attitudes, aspirations, and other psychological criteria that define a person.

Let's divide psychographics into two buckets: frustrations and fears, and wants and aspirations.

Frustrations and Fears

Your *customer avatar* has some kind of pain today, and they're likely trying to move away from that pain and toward a goal or vision of the future. You want to capture that.

Possible problems:

- I'm not attracting enough leads and customers to my business.

- I don't have the time or interest to market my business.

- My prospective clients don't know enough about our process for us to sell to them.

Considering these broad problem statements, answer this question: What specific frustrations and fears does your avatar have?

They might look like this:

- I'm afraid we're going to miss payroll again because we don't have any leads coming in.

- My partners hate doing business development, and it's driving me crazy.

- I'm sick and tired of staying at the office late and missing out on my time with family.

- I don't have the time to invest in marketing my business.

- I lack confidence in digital marketing agencies because the last company promised the world and delivered nothing.

- I waste the first hour of every new client meeting discussing basics about our firm.

As you can see, I took broad market problems and applied them to an individual. You can do the same, and you should. Writing about general audience problems is better than doing nothing but writing to an avatar's frustrations and fears will make your content come to life.

 **Generalists thrive on the idea that anyone's a client–they love solving new problems every time. This is the same as treading water.**

Wants and Aspirations

You can also look at your avatar's problems and "flip" them to positive statements:

- I want to get back to growing my business and having fun again.

- I wish I had a steady stream of new prospective clients to meet with.

- I wish the world could see and learn about the great work our firm is doing.

- I want to leave the office by 5 p.m. every day.

- I want to find a reliable digital marketing company that can help us grow and compete.

- I want to earn a top award for the work we're doing; our firm and people deserve recognition.

- I want to sell my firm within the next ten years and travel the world with my husband; maybe even write a book.

You may notice in this list of wants and aspirations how little I wrote about the solutions a digital agency might provide. That's because building a customer avatar isn't about your ideal customer's thoughts on your services. It's about creating a real-life character, and no one in real life wants a website—or Facebook campaign—they want something else much deeper and personal. Zeroing in on your customer avatar is going to help you tap into that *personal* element—which will help your material take on a life of its own.

Purchasing Drivers

The final part of creating your customer avatar will involve thinking about why they buy. Purchasing drivers are a form of psychographics, but you should focus on them specifically to make sure you consider why your customer will make an investment in your services.

For the avatar I've been working on in this chapter, those reasons could look like this:

- I want to invest in growing my architecture firm.

- I am ready to build up the credibility of my firm in the Denver community.

- I'm tired of seeing my competition growing their firms and leaving me in the dust.

- I need someone to do the marketing for us.
- I can't afford a large upfront investment but could probably handle a marketing retainer.
- I need to get my partners to buy in on any major business decision.

We now have a good picture of *why* our avatar might want to buy digital marketing services.

Putting It All Together

Now you've thought about demographics, psychographics, and purchasing drivers. Next, edit your lists to pull out the best elements of the work you've done so far. Also, consider adding a photo to help you visualize your character even better (and give it one more personal touch)—check out Exhibit 4 for an example.

Exhibit 4

Jill the Architect

- ☐ Partner at a 10-person $2.5m/yr firm
- ☐ 42 years-old
- ☐ Married with two children
- ☐ I'm afraid we're going to miss payroll again because we don't have any leads coming in.
- ☐ I'm sick and tired of staying at the office later and missing out on my time with my family.
- ☐ I don't have time to invest in marketing my business.
- ☐ I want to invest in growing my architecture firm
- ☐ I am ready to build up the credibility of my firm in the Denver community.
- ☐ I'm tired of seeing my competition growing their firms and leaving me in the dust.
- ☐ I need someone to do the marketing for us.
- ☐ I need to get my architecture firm partners to buy-in on any major business decisions

How cool is that? You've gone from selling to architects to selling to Jill! For more help with this process, download the Get Rich In The Deep End Field Guide at ownyourmarket.com/guide.

 Owning your market brings respect, desirability, authority, process, demand, scale, predictability, clarity, and simplicity.

What to Do Next

Who are you trying to attract as a customer to your business? How do they think of themselves? Do they organize in the narrow way you've defined with your customer segment—or are they part of a larger group of people?

When it comes to audience, customer segment is your starting point—but you'll probably need to open up" your definition a bit to help you find relevant awareness channels. More on those later in this book.

It often helps to cast a wider net so your message can resonate with the right people in your primary and secondary audiences. After all, you're not trying to attract 100% of *any* audience—you want the *right* people who are most likely to buy. Moving out from your customer segment to identify primary and secondary audiences requires a bit of thinking, but it's not too hard.

For instance, if this is your customer segment:

- Architects
  - \> $1 million in annual revenue
  - Five-plus team members
  - Operating in Colorado
  - Currently invest in digital advertising

Your primary audience might simply be "architects," or even "self-employed architects." And don't discount the possibility that you might have multiple audiences that contain the same customer segment.

For example, the UGURUS customer segment is:

- Digital agency owner
  - Entrepreneur
  - Less than ten employees
  - Full time in their business
  - Speak English fluently

Very few audiences out there are this targeted. We use this customer segment information to identify secondary audiences that might contain some of our ideal customers. That means that while "digital agency owners" is our primary audience, we have several relevant secondary audiences:

- Web designers and developers
- Digital marketers
- Entrepreneurs

Speaking to all three of these audiences helps us to reach the customer segment we've defined, even though not every person in each of these secondary audiences is a good match.

As you gain momentum, you'll likely outgrow or saturate certain audiences. You'll also be constantly learning about your market, and this process will open up new ideas for you about audiences where your ideal customer hangs out.

Over time, you can continue to add audience groups to your MarketMap to help you find more and more audiences—and their supporting infrastructure—to build awareness for your company and the services and products you offer.

Chapter Five Take Aways to Get Rich In The Deep End

- ◆ The best target markets self-identify as the market. You've already lost if you have to explain to someone that they fit in your market.

- ◆ Your niche should self-identify themselves. Doctors, dentists, coaches, WordPress users, seven-figure entrepreneurs, digital agency owners–these people know they belong to these groups. If you can align your target market in this way, it makes things so much easier.

- ◆ Secondary audiences are larger markets and complementary markets that have some of your ideal clients.

- ◆ Niche success happens at the intersection of money, interest, and results. Does your market have money and are they willing to spend it? Does the market interest you? Passion will come later. Can you get them results?

- ◆ Tapping into other people's audiences is the fastest way to put your message in front of hundreds, thousands, or even millions of people overnight.

- ◆ Talk about your ideal client's pain better than they understand it and they will instantly see you as an expert to solve their problems.

CHAPTER SIX

Heather Builds Awareness

When Heather and I met again at the café, I could hardly wait to check in with her on her homework. Sure, I was excited to see the headlines she had come up with. But I was more interested in whether her mindset about her competitor had changed.

I didn't have to wait long to find out. Before Heather set her latte on the table, she was updating me.

"I spoke with the owner of Course Launch! Her name is Tamela. She doesn't actually do the web and marketing side for the online courses they build. They're more of an instructional design company, and they use subcontractors to build the web components. Then they hand off the projects to other agencies to help their clients' market.

"They also work with a lot of other markets—not just coaches. We're talking about potentially being able to collaborate since I'm not big on instructional design."

Then she looked at me with a sheepish grin on her face. "It's okay. You can say it."

"What?" I smiled. "'I told you so'? I would never say that."

Over coffee, Heather told me she had never considered her competitors as allies and friends. She'd never imagined that other agency owners could be leveraged as collaborative partners. Heather admitted that she thought the call with Tamela was going to be painful and competitive. In reality, it was friendly and full of energy.

They had agreed to schedule a follow-up call in a couple of weeks to talk more specifics on what their collaboration might look like. Tamela even thanked her for reaching out, telling Heather she'd been waiting to meet someone just like her.

I enjoyed seeing Heather's beliefs about what was possible for her business change before my eyes.

"Heather," I said, "congratulations on making this bold move, but you're not done yet. To niche your business and own your market, you'll have to get comfortable with doing the uncomfortable – just like jumping into the deep end of dark waters where you can't see the bottom. For instance, I'm going to need you to find ten new publishers in your niche to pitch all of those fresh headlines ideas to."

Heather replied with gritted teeth.

"I was actually thinking I would publish this content on my own blog, I've been meaning to update my site, and I bet this would get me some good search engine exposure."

I reminded Heather of her previous success with someone else's platform. "Remember how you tapped into the audience Amy had already built? Amy's blog is an awareness channel.

"Pretend you're a rock band that's just starting out, trying to get gigs at venues all around town. The Beatles spent three years playing on every stage they could—from Liverpool, England to Hamburg, Germany—before they finally convinced someone to give them a record deal.

"Be like the Beatles. Start 'gigging' to build awareness in your market.

"So, how about those publishers?"

I could see Heather's stomach churn. "I just need to do what you say in the Field Guide, right?"

"You got it, Heather."

And with that, our coffee was done. Heather left to start researching available publishers in the business coaching market. Over the next week, she did a few Google searches and also reached out to Amy for insight. To her surprise, Amy mentioned several websites that Heather didn't find through the search engines.

Suddenly, Heather had a list of almost a dozen publishers—along with a handful of influencer blogs, podcasts, and industry-focused social media groups.

Heather later told me that when it came time to email the first publisher, she almost had a breakdown. She had always hated reaching out to people she didn't know—she was never a fan of cold calling or sending unsolicited email—and here I was forcing her to get up close and personal. I encouraged her to stick with the method and scripts that were outlined in the exercises I gave her—which are outlined in this book.

In the end, she copied and pasted the scripts into her email workflow. Then she grabbed a couple of headline concepts and made slight changes to each email to personalize the messages she was sending.

Later on, Heather confessed she sat on the first email for several minutes—just staring at the screen without being able to hit "send." She said she was imagining the inconvenience she was causing the person on the other end. And she was sure that she was about to be rejected.

But she did it, and I'm proud of her. So much of learning to step out into an audience of people is about working with fear, not against it. It doesn't matter whether it's on a stage, on a podcast, or on a blog.

The difference-maker, Heather said, was a quote by Steven Pressfield that I had mentioned: "The amateur believes he must first overcome his fear; then he can do his work. The professional knows that fear can never be overcome."[6]

And so Heather held her breath and pressed the send button. And suddenly it was done.

She couldn't believe she had stepped so far outside of her comfort zone. She didn't even know any of the people at these blogs—but she committed to follow the recipe I outlined in the Field Guide anyway.

After sending the first pitch email, her resistance faded. She queued up another pitch email and then another. To her surprise, each subsequent email got more comfortable to write and send. She sent out all of her headline ideas to ten publishers within about twenty minutes.

Then, before she even closed her inbox, she got her first proper rejection from the top publisher in the coaching market: "Thank you for reaching out, but these articles aren't a good fit for our audience."

And there it was. With a sinking feeling, Heather realized she'd been right all along. The only surprise was how quickly her fears had been validated.

Rejection?

By the time Heather and I met for coffee again, she had received three more rejection emails—and I could tell she was frustrated.

I broke the silence. "So you got four total rejections and then what? Maybe six publishers haven't gotten back to you yet?"

Heather took a sip of her latte. "No, two others got back to me and said they liked one of the headlines. But now they want me to write the articles so they can review before they agree to publish."

My eyes lit up. "Heather! This is great news. You have two more publishers coming online! You just multiplied your audience and awareness channels by 200%!"

Apparently, this hadn't occurred to Heather. I could see the gears turning in her head. "I never thought about it like that. It's just that I was rejected by so many and didn't hear back from others. I guess I thought they were all going to accept my content the way that Amy had."

I nodded and tried to reassure her. "Heather, don't worry about it. They're just names on a list. The reason we build a list is you're going to get rejected. If rejection weren't a part of this, then we would just identify one publisher or channel at a time.

"But that's not the case. You will get rejected.

"So we use the power of a list to overcome that fact. The goal is to get access to new audiences. Rejection is proof that you're working your list.

"Rejection is a great thing. Truly."

Now, Heather hadn't realized it yet, but as she stepped further and further into owning her market, many of the people who had "rejected" her would eventually come to accept her content. Often, getting rejected is just the first step in getting accepted.

Rejection, to use a baseball metaphor, is a sign that you're taking swings. And the more you swing, the stronger you'll get—and the more likely it is that you'll eventually hit the ball out of the park.

"Heather, now I'm going to let you in on a secret: patient persistence. Can you pull up one of the emails you sent to a publisher that has yet to respond?"

I explained to Heather what life looks like for a typical editor. How they're caught between the publisher's pressure to drive ad revenue, membership, or sales—and still stay on top of the editor's job of building a consistent, high-quality pipeline of great content that satisfies their readers.

Many of them are busy, understaffed, and unable to respond to every pitch that comes in their inbox. And at some publications, the same person wears both the editor's and publisher's hats!

 **Rejection is proof you're taking action.**

So when we're pitching, we need to make their jobs easier. Yes, we might need to use a metaphorical hammer to break through their initial "no"—but that hammer needs to be covered in velvet, so to speak. And we're going to use that velvet hammer to tap instead of smash.

In other words, we need to be gracious and humble in every interaction. We need to aim to help them by getting them great content and staying at the top of their inbox.

But we're not going to give up until we hear a flat-out "No, don't ever talk to us again." I walked Heather through a simple follow-up email script—just a one-sentence addition to her original email.

Heather resisted. "But I just emailed them last week! I don't want to bother them."

"Heather," I explained, "we have to change that belief. You're not bothering them. You're helping them.

"You have content—high-quality content—that their audience needs.

"All you need them to do is allow you to help them."

Heather hesitated for a moment. But since she had her laptop with her, she opened it up. Then she wrote the politely persistent follow-up and hit send—and sent three more to other publishers as well! "Can't wait for more rejection!"

I laughed—and then remembered one more thing. "Oh, and Heather—that number one publisher that turned your content ideas down. Let's take a look at some of their most popular articles and see if we can come up with some fresh ideas to resubmit.

"Getting them to publish you would be a game-changer, so we're going to keep trying."

She tensed. "You mean you want me to get rejected again?"

"Yep. Even if it takes fifty rejections. It's worth that much to have their name and traffic working for your business."

Then Heather and I crafted a "thank you for the rejection" email that showed appreciation for the constructive feedback, let them know we researched their publication further, and suggested a few more headline ideas.

I was feeling pretty excited for her—but I had no idea what was about to come. By the time I got home from the coffee shop, Heather had already forwarded me a message from one of the unresponsive publishers:

Heather! I apologize for not getting back to you sooner. I was sharing your content ideas with Emily, my editor, and we don't want to choose one—we want all three. Just send over the content and we'll queue it up in our publishing calendar.

Emily and I agreed that the "ultimate guide" you showed us is just the type of rich content our audience would like to see more of.

By the way, we are also in the process of launching a new influencer program where we will be publishing a monthly article from a group of experts. Let us know if you would be interested in helping us with this project.

—Frank

As you can imagine, Heather was feeling pretty fantastic to be called an influencer so quickly in her new market.

So there it was. After just a few emails, Heather now had access to four awareness channels in her audience—empowering her to put her message in front of thousands and thousands of potential clients.

 **Awareness only matters if it drives conversations.**

These relationships would open doors for Heather that stretched far beyond just the blogs they publish. Because each publisher also had email lists, and partnerships with industry influencers, and their own reputation within the market she served. Some even held conferences, ran podcasts, and had many other awareness opportunities that Heather might be able to leverage in the future—by merely building her relationship with them by providing high-quality, valuable content.

For Heather, the old world—the one in which she waited by the phone, hoping it would ring—was already becoming a distant memory.

Heather was starting to own her market.

Chapter Six Take Aways to Get Rich In The Deep End

◆ The Beatles didn't get famous from playing in their garage. They gigged. They played seven nights a week sometimes two or three times a night all over Liverpool and Hamburg before coming to the states and becoming "overnight successes." Be the Beatles, not the garage band.

◆ The world needs your help. If you're holding back a solution from clients and your market, that's pretty selfish. It's your duty to reach out to as many people in your market and let them know how you can help.

◆ Getting rejected from publishers and media is proof your reaching out. Measuring the number of rejections is a better way to gauge your commitment than successes.

◆ Use the power of a list to overcome rejection. If one in twenty says yes, then it only takes sixty people on your list to get published three times. These three wins could put you in front of a hundred thousand people. That's the power of rejection.

◆ Following up with people is not bothering them. You are serving them by making it easy for them to get back to you.

◆ Rejection isn't permanent. If a top publisher or connection in your market says no, re-pitch them again in the future. The best outlets are worth fifty rejections.

CHAPTER SEVEN

The Second A—Awareness

Now that you have a deep understanding of your audience, it's time to make them aware that you exist. That's the second A in the 5-A Framework: Awareness.

Most agencies—in fact, most companies—rely solely on referrals and word of mouth. Those can be powerful ways to get leads, but they're slow and arduous, and they can be challenging to control. However, creating awareness *yourself* works like word of mouth on steroids. To do that, you need two things: channels and activities.

Awareness channels are ways to reach your audience and market. Publishers, associations, strategic partners, or groups that contain members of your audience—these are all awareness channels.

If you already have an audience, list, or fan-base, you could consider your own website and blog as awareness channels, too.

Awareness activities are events or tactics that put your message in front of the awareness channels you're targeting. Activities can be articles, interviews, keynote presentations, or anything else that gets your message out.

 **Marketing shouldn't be disconnected, random tactics. It should be an engine that you can put your foot on the gas and get a predictable and reliable result for your business.**

In the last chapter, you read how Heather had been leveraging online blogs and publishers to build awareness with content. Each publisher was a channel Heather could use to reach her audience. Each article was an activity that communicated her message to the channel.

You need to do this work, just like Heather did—because making your market aware of you is a vital and necessary step in owning your market. You could be the most talented in the space you serve, but if no one knows that, your talents don't matter.

Not all awareness is created equal, though. There are likely many awareness channels in your market: blogs, podcasts, webinars, conferences, stages, but some are less effective than others.

For example, an article can get you exposure to hundreds, maybe even thousands, of people from your audience—and you can write it from the comfort of your office.

Speaking on stage, on the other hand, might only put you in front of dozens or hundreds of people from your audience. Plus, a speech typically requires a lot more preparation, and you need to travel to engage your audience. However, a well-executed talk can usually build a lot more credibility in a shorter amount of time.

Whether that means speaking on stage is more valuable to you than writing an article is a personal choice. There is no "one way" to build your following within your market. Every market will have a different mix of channels and activities available to you, which means you'll have to evaluate what's right for *you*.

How to Create Awareness

Much of building awareness is about leveraging awareness channels—either one you own or a channel that someone else owns. I'll talk about awareness activities throughout this chapter and the book, but channels deserve special attention, so I want to focus on those.

An "owned" awareness channel is an asset that you have control over where you can build *your* audience. You're the one who determines when and how your message appears—with very few obstacles or filters. (Think of your website, your email list, your own Facebook group, or your YouTube channel.)

Someone else's channel, on the other hand, is one you don't own. Instead of building your audience, you can only use it to *leverage an audience that already exists.*

When you want to use someone else's channel for awareness, you'll be at the mercy of another entrepreneur, editor, or influencer. You'll encounter higher standards and obstacles around getting your message on the platform.

But leveraging that audience can be extremely helpful to you—which means trying to get access to other people's channels is worth the work.

So which should you do—build your own audience or leverage someone else's? Exhibit 5 shows a comparison of the two options.

Exhibit 5

BUILD YOUR AUDIENCE	LEVERAGE EXISTING AUDIENCE
☐ Self-Publish (blog, magazine, podcast, social, etc.) ☐ Email list ☐ Groups (Facebook, LinkedIn, etc.)	☐ Get published (blog, magazine, podcast, associations, stages) ☐ PPC / Ads to audience members ☐ Sponsored content (blogs, lists, etc.)
Pros	**Pros**
☐ Build an "owned media" asset that you can repeatedly get in front of ☐ Enjoy the audience long-term, with a high potential return on investment (but no guarantees) ☐ Take advantage of a low barrier to your awareness activities — and no publishing lag	☐ Use and existing audience (i.e., someone else's hard work) ☐ Access the audence on a one-off basis, with a lower but more reliable return on investment ☐ Get valuable market feedback
Cons	**Cons**
☐ In the short-term, get a meager return on your inverstment ☐ Get very little guidance on market validation	☐ Struggle with publishing lag (you have no control over publishing time) ☐ Harder hurdles to clear around quality and app

You can see in the diagram in Exhibit 5, I listed "stage" as a form of being published. Yes, I realize that no one is "publishing" you when you stand up on a stage and speak, but for the sake of convenience, I talk exclusively about publishers, publishing, and getting published. I refer to the act of getting in front of any awareness channel as being "published."

Why It's Better to Publish on Existing Channels

There's a reason I talked to Heather about the Beatles—because thinking of a rock band is a great way to understand awareness.

Your garage is a lousy place to build an audience for your band. When you're starting out or trying to gain traction, you need to go to the places where your potential fans are.

Yes, it's scary as hell to send your audition video to a local pub, but that fear will push you to level up your game. You can badly play Stairway to Heaven as many times as you want at home—but performing in front of an audience is a different process. It forces you to practice and get better.

You'll need to impress the pub manager first, though—and she might even say no. Then you'll have to practice some more. Finally, you'll be ready for the bright lights and—hopefully—enjoy some applause.

Then, as you get better, you'll get the opportunity to perform for bigger and bigger existing audiences. You'll open for a headliner. And after enough gigs, you'll begin to have fans of your own, and a following that will help you grow into the big time.

Make sense?

Good, because it's not just rock bands that go through this process. You need to do the same thing with your business—only each "pub" is an awareness channel, and each "gig" is an awareness activity.

Yes, it's *possible* to circumvent this whole process. You *can* build an audience slowly by investing 100% of your efforts into your own platform, but that will be a painfully slow process.

A lot of people think they have to start there and do the hard work, but that's not true. Don't fall for the lie that existing channels are unavailable to you because you're not yet "good enough" to be published. For proof, you don't have to look any further than my own story.

When we first launched the UGURUS website, we had four blog posts, a single lead magnet, and no homepage. But instead of getting too caught up in who we were and what we planned on selling, we instead focused on *building up an audience* of people interested in our message.

We leveraged existing blogs that boasted over 100,000 monthly visitors—and, in some cases, up to 1,000,000. These publishers helped us get massive exposure, fast.

Exhibit 6

Now, not every market will have this type of infrastructure available, but isn't it worth finding out if yours does?

How to Get Published on Existing Channels

Almost every channel with an existing audience has a problem: the publisher needs an endless supply of high-quality content to keep their business alive. And they have two big fears: 1) that the next piece of content they publish will miss the mark and their audience will flee, and 2) that they won't *have* another piece of content around the corner and their publishing schedule will fall apart.

The thing is, publishers rarely have time to go out and recruit new talent, so they look to others like them that have accepted content; this gives them pre-validation on what content might work well for them. This means they typically do one of the following:

- Respond to only some of the people who pitch them, if any at all.

- Consider people they know in their own network.

- Leverage their network to connect with others.

- Look at who else is publishing people.

It will be *most helpful* for you to get published on a channel that has a lot of traffic—so don't stop trying to find the "who's who" in your space and getting published there. But it's not a waste of your time—at all—to get published by someone even if they don't have a big audience. Getting published by *anyone* that has authority in your market, no matter what size their audience is, will help you build momentum.

Here's the best part: you only need to get published once to get the ball rolling. Once you've been published that first time, the chances of others doing the same go up exponentially.

Finding Publishers

I use two methods to find publishers with audiences.

First, I start with Google, searching for terms like:

"[your market] blog"

"[your market] podcast"

"how to grow a [your market] business"

When you find some ideas, add their names to your MarketMap and pursue whatever you find. Follow all leads! Nothing is too small or insignificant.

For example, I was once on a call with a client when we found a top podcast in her niche. On the "About" page for the podcast, they listed the four different hosts of the program and their Twitter handles. Following those links led us to their own websites, blogs, and businesses—and each had multiple publishing channels that would accept guest content.

When I'm done with Google, I use my second method—I ask people in my market where they go to learn, who they follow, and if they know who's out there publishing. You can try this one-on-one, in-person, remotely, even over email in a survey.

Push beyond ridiculous answers (e.g., "I don't know, sorry"). Take the time to see what they really mean. "Come on, that can't be true. Isn't there one person in this market that you follow?"

If you belong to any social media groups in your niche, consider asking in a post: "Who are the top names in this industry? What blogs do you follow? What podcasts do you listen to? What books do you read?"

It doesn't take very long to build an exhaustive MarketMap of publishers in your niche. You'll slowly add to the list over time, but most markets have many effective channels. Once you start hearing the same names you already have on your list, you'll know you have a good starting point.

Remember, though: not every publisher is a *great* publisher. The best ones have a large(ish) audience built in. While you're researching, try to find proof that the websites, podcasts, and stages you're discovering have a good-sized audience.

Websites that are supported by advertising will usually boast about their viewership on their advertiser info pages. Just go to the footer of the site and look for a link to advertisers, or something similar.

With podcasts, you can guess at the audience size by looking at the number of reviews they have, and the number of episodes they've produced.

Stages? Read the website and you'll often find clues like: "Join over 400 architects at the industry's largest annual gathering."

Of course, there is a *context* for audience size. A publisher could say they have tens of thousands on an email list—and still not get much traffic to their blog or video channel. Browse through their articles and posts. See if you can get a feel for engagement. Are there comments? Are there social shares? Some sites even share a public view count.

If you can find the total "reach" of a publisher you're interested in, add that to your MarketMap.

Next, rank your publishers in tiers. Getting published by lower-tier publishers is usually easier. You'll be leveraging smaller awareness channels, but this step might be necessary before you can make it to the top names in your niche.

Don't get me wrong, though—that shouldn't stop you from reaching out to your top-tier publishers. Depending on your market, you might be able to get published by the top names on your first try.

There's only one way to find out: just do it.

 **Repeat your core message often. It'll take at least 7 times before your audience hears anything for the first time.**

Getting Accepted

If you can't find information on a publisher's site about how to get access to their platform—info on whether they accept guest posts, or how to apply to speak, for example—your next best bet is to ask them.

An email that looks like this is a good place to start:

Subject: Interested in learning more...

Body:

Hey [firstname/company/etc.]—

I've been following [their publication name] for a bit and was wondering what it takes to publish on your platform. Do you accept content from guest contributors?

Here's that same formula, but soliciting a speaking opportunity:

Subject: Interested in learning more...

Body:

Hello [firstname/company/etc.]—

I've recently discovered [event name] and it looks fantastic.

I was wondering what it takes to speak on your stage. Do you accept pitches?

Or, you can send an email with specific headline ideas:

Subject: Potential articles for your website?

Body:

Hey [firstname/company/etc.]—

I read over your guest contributor guidelines, and I came up with three article ideas you might be interested in:

Headline 1

Headline 2

Headline 3

I want to make sure I provide the angle to help your publication in the best way I can. Would you be interested in any of the above? If not, let me know a different idea you think would resonate better.

Or, if you have proven authority in the market:

Subject: Potential podcast appearance

Body:

Hey [firstname/company/etc.]—

I've been a fan of your podcast for a while, and I came up with three interview ideas you might be interested in:

Headline 1

Headline 2

Headline 3

I want to make sure I come up with the best idea for an engaging interview your listeners would enjoy. Would you be interested in talking about any of the above? If not, let me know a different angle you think would resonate better.

Here are three other podcasts I've recently done:

Podcast 1

Podcast 2

Podcast 3

If you're unsure about what ideas you should pitch, think about your audience's top three problems, and consider your top three solutions. Mix and match these together and you're sure to come up with some ideas.

You can even look to news sites like *USA Today* to get a handle on what's popular at the moment. Here are some headlines I wrote in just a couple of minutes for a dental audience:

- "7 Mistakes Your Dental Practice Might Be Making on Your Website"
- "How to Find New Patients Online with One Simple Change"
- "Save 1 Hour of Administrative Work Every Week by Doing This"
- "The Truth About Why Your Website Isn't Working for Your Practice"
- "What Donald Trump Taught Me About Digital Marketing for Dentists"

As you can imagine, your ideas need to be interesting. However, they don't have to be the best ones in the world. You're looking for a publisher to see something and agree—or to give you constructive feedback on what might connect better with their audience. You taking action and making contact with publishers—imperfectly— is more important than opining over the perfect pitch email. Take *imperfect action*.

Good publishers with professional editors often have a few ideas of their own that they know their readers are hungry for. Producing whatever they ask of you is a great way to build a relationship. Then, once you've built up some relationship capital, you'll have more freedom around getting your ideas accepted.

And remember—these steps are identical no matter the channel. If I were pitching conference organizers on a topic for a keynote, I would do the same thing: give them a few ideas for the talk and get their feedback.

Podcast? Same thing: build a relationship with the host and laser in on an angle they think would resonate with their audience.

Dealing with Rejection

I often tell people that when we first started UGURUS and I was contacting publishers, I reached out to twenty-five of them. I got twenty-two "no thank you's." That's a whole lot of rejection. But knowing that you'll face inevitable rejection shouldn't depress you in the slightest. In fact, it should invigorate you.

If you see a competitor in your market getting some success, it's not because someone came to them one morning and said, "You're so awesome and better than anyone else. Can you write an article for us? Can you speak on our stage?"

It's because they made contact with a publisher, built a relationship, pitched an idea, and—very likely—overcame a lot of "no's." As it turned out, I personally didn't need twenty-five publishers to publish my work.

Three said yes right away, and three of the original "no's" later came back and accepted posts once we showed them others had published. When we had those six, our market authority kicked in— and most of the rest that had said no accepted our requests.

Producing Your Content

Once a publisher has said yes to an idea, angle, or topic, you need to develop your content. I'll dive into a winning content framework later in this book, but the main thing to remember at this stage is that you need to *meet or exceed whatever agreement you established with your publisher.* Hit your deadline, stay in communication, and be flexible.

To that end, when you send them the finished product, I would soft pitch it as a "draft" and say you are open to their feedback. (However, don't think that "draft" means you can cut corners, or submit a piece of work that you know needs editing. Your draft should be your best work, given your time and resources.)

If you can, have at least one good writer review your work and help you with clarity and grammar. If you don't know anyone who can review your content, consider hiring an editor. Aaron Wrixon, this book's co-author, helped me in drafting a preliminary version of this book, and is well worth the investment. He's set up a special "Hello" page for you at wrixon.com/ownyourmarket.If you can't pay for help, do your best to edit on your own. Try the Grammarly app that checks your work using artificial intelligence, or an app like Hemingway that offers suggestions to make your writing clearer and more concise. Or see if you can have a friend or colleague give it a look over.

When the publisher gives feedback, take it positively and constructively. They know their audience better than you do, so if they ask for a tweak or change, do your best to comply and make it better.

Some of my clients take constructive feedback as rejection. It's not. Even if it's delivered harshly, *any* kind of feedback from a publisher represents an opportunity to improve. Make the changes and send your revised material back for another round of approval.

As long as a publisher is engaged with you, you are in the game and making progress.

Promoting Your Content

Once your publisher has accepted your content, you'll have to wait to see the fruits of your labor. If it's a blog post being published or podcast interview, this could mean a few days—or possibly weeks or months. I've waited for content to go live for more than six months.

But once your content *is* published, do your best to draw as much attention to it as possible. Share it on social media. Email your list. Get the word out. If you are speaking at an event, promote it.

If the content is public, like on a blog or on a podcast, engage with the audience. Answer questions people ask in the blog post comments. Reply to tweets. Review the podcast and say how awesome it was for you to be a guest.

In short, do everything you can to call attention to your great work—just as if it was published on your very own website. This will help you leverage this piece of content for your own audience, and it will set you up for success with the publisher in the future.

That level of relationship is essential because once you've been accepted by a publisher, you have a better chance of working with them on a regular schedule. That makes the whole process go much smoother and faster.

I have publisher relationships where I drop an email to them once a month with headline ideas, they respond, and I write. That means I'm never worried about whether they'll get back to me. (Which, let me tell you, is a welcomed thing.)

 **Even the smallest opportunity can lead to something big. Follow all leads.**

Being Consistent

Not every awareness activity gets you in front of an entire channel—let alone your whole audience.

Many factors limit your reach:

- Timing
- Platform
- Reach
- Persistence
- Content and context

Many people who get published, however, do it once and then check it off their to-do list. This approach is like wanting to get in shape for a beach-front vacation and going to the gym only one time.

That single workout could have been the most amazing ever witnessed in the history of the human race—but it will have almost zero impact on your outward appearance. If you only work out once, you'll be left with a sore body and very little in terms of tangible results.

Working out becomes valuable only if you do it consistently. The second time to the gym, your body will be slightly more ready and willing, and you'll feel less sore afterward. Twenty workouts later, you'll start to see a visible change in your appearance. All of a sudden, looking good on the beach is not only possible—you are starting to see it happen.

Awareness is the same. Chances are, the first time your audience hears or sees your content, they might not know what to think about you or your message.

To build awareness, you need to keep going—and do it often. Remember, if the Beatles had stopped after one gig, they wouldn't have become the greatest rock band in history.

Building Momentum

In our modern society, we're exposed to anywhere from five hundred to five thousand advertisements per day. No wonder we feel so distracted all the time!

Part of cutting through all of that noise? Putting out high-quality information about the problems you solve. But here's an equally important part—doing it repeatedly. To compete, you must be consistent and persistent.

There's an old advertising adage that you need to show your customer your message seven times before they "see it" for the first time.

If you consider that idea—and remember that not every article or keynote you deliver will reach the entire audience you are targeting—you can see that you'll have to do a lot of awareness activities before you can thoroughly saturate your market.

This reality could overwhelm you. You might think, "How am I ever going to tell *everyone* in my market about me?"

But don't let the need to repeatedly get your message in front of your audience bother you—let it inspire you. There's a lot of opportunity in your market, and there are customers who are waiting for your help. How many of those customers do you actually *need* for your business to be successful?

It doesn't matter whether you want ten or twenty new clients per year—or fifty. Every awareness activity will put you in front of some percentage of your market and contribute to the results you need.

I often compare the process to watching snow pile up. Each single awareness activity is like a snowflake: unique, but inconsequential. Yet when enough snow accumulates, an avalanche breaks—and unimaginable energy is unleashed.

It's too easy to get an article accepted or a keynote speech commitment and breathe a sigh of relief, to say, "Well, I did it," and then call it a day. Instead, as soon as you send a finished article to a publisher, immediately start on the next one. If a conference just accepted your keynote presentation, submit the same pitch to five more organizations and conferences.

There's nothing quite like sending this in an email to leverage the social herd mentality that humans are hardwired for: "So-and-so just booked me for their annual conference where I'm going to be talking about XYZ. This topic is in such demand right now, I know their members are going to eat it up. I was curious about your upcoming conference. Are you still accepting presentation pitches?"

Remember: this process is about building momentum, so don't wait until your article is published or your keynote presentation is delivered. There will be *way* too much time in between activities to maintain that momentum.

So pile up those snowflakes—and get ready for the avalanche.

When and How to Build Your Own Audience

There is no hard and fast rule about when to start taking advantage of your own publishing platform. In your early days of owning your market, I'd recommend that you spend less than half of your marketing time on your own platform. Maybe even *much* less than half.

Although you might see more followers on social media and more cold traffic coming to your website, that traffic doesn't really amount to much.

For starters, you don't really "own" your social media. Many businesses had a rude awakening when Facebook changed their algorithm and made it harder for companies to share organic content. Overnight, businesses were forced to fork over ad dollars if they wanted to reach their followers.

Search traffic isn't much better because you have no guarantee that Google will continue to favor your content over someone else's. Many publishers have experienced abrupt downturns in traffic due to Google updates.

But even when you get published on someone else's channel, you're really only borrowing traffic. The trick is to convert all of this traffic into *truly* owned media. You'll learn how later in the book.

Whatever you do, however, consider limiting the number of channels you own. When publishing on other channels, you need to go where the audience is, but when publishing on your own channels, less is better. Spreading your attention across five or six of your own channels dilutes your efforts.

I'd rather see you turn a single channel into a powerful asset than spread yourself thin, trying to keep up with everything. Remember: if the best place to find content from you is email, people will subscribe to your email list. Your fans will follow you wherever you are.

Finally, when you do start to see some traction building your own audience, remember that it's a long-game activity. You'll often get bursts of opportunity by publishing on someone else's platform, but when it comes to your own platform, you have to nurture slowly—and then nurture some more.

If you plan to blog on your site, determine a realistic commitment over the long run. Is it a post per week—or only one per month? If you plan to launch a podcast, can you maintain an episode every week for the next five years? That's over 260 episodes!

When you're building up your own awareness channels, consistency wins the day. Decide on an achievable frequency and then stick to it. The road to success on the internet is littered with good intentions. People say, "I'm going to post every day!" Then four years later they're looking at the last post they wrote—four years ago.

I know about this experience because I've lived it. Dozens of times. I can tell you from the trenches that the most successful content publishing campaigns we ever ran—the ones that had the most impact on our business—were the ones that were done consistently over the long term.

Make things easy on yourself. Choose one or two channels to own (e.g., email, blog and email, blog and Facebook, etc.), and select an interval that you can maintain for years.

If you have a burst of productivity one week, build a buffer. There are times when I have six or seven weeks of our podcast in the can. There are other times where I fall behind, and every week is turned around just in time.

I can tell you which times I prefer.

Chapter Seven Take Aways to Get Rich In The Deep End

- Most agencies are really good at what they do. The problem is, no one knows about them. They aren't sharing their story and results with their market. It's 100% your responsibility to take ownership over this. You have to be your best evangelist.

- Making your audience aware of you is a vital and necessary step in owning your market.

- When it comes to building awareness for your agency, start with existing audiences. Building your own audience is great, but time consuming. The shortcut is to start with what's already available.

- Once you get published the first time, the chance it will happen a second and third time goes up exponentially.

- When it comes to gaining momentum in your market, even the smallest opportunity can lead to something big. Follow all leads.

- No one wants to be the "first" outlet to give someone new a chance. Even if your first opportunity is small potatoes, it will help you get your next.

◆ Rejection shouldn't demoralize you. In fact, it should invigorate you.

◆ When it comes to publishers or stages, you don't need 25 to say "yes," just one can set you up with all of the clients you need for the next year.

◆ Don't play to win all of them. Play to win the next.

◆ Never pitch completed work. Whether an article or talk. Pitch the headline. Sell the elevator pitch. The high-level concept. Get agreement on the idea first, then do the work of creation.

◆ Treat every blog post, interview, or talk like a graduation announcement. Tell the world. Let people know. Shout that thing from rooftops.

◆ Producing content for your awareness channels is more like a fitness routine. One workout–no matter how epic– won't get you the results you're looking for. Consistency, persistency, and pushing yourself to do better and improve will get you what you're after.

◆ Pile your awareness activities like snowflakes on a mountain. With enough hits, it'll create an avalanche of momentum for your business.

◆ Spend less than half of your marketing time building your own audience. The rest should be spent working with existing audiences.

◆ You don't need 50 marketing channels. One or two will likely get you the results you need–with consistent activity.

CHAPTER EIGHT

Heather Learns How to Attract Her Audience

Heather and I took our usual table looking out onto Colfax, a busy, eclectic avenue in downtown Denver. I could sense something was wrong—and not just because she appeared to be more interested in what was going on outside the café than in her own business. After some small talk, Heather let me in on what was troubling her.

"That publisher rejected me again. Remember? The top one in the business coaching market. They said something about how they don't publish this type of content, which of course isn't true. We scanned through their blog before we submitted those titles! I just don't get it."

I nodded. "You're right, Heather. It never feels good getting rejected, but we talked about this. What is rejection again?"

A smile cracked across Heather's face. "Proof that we're taking action."

"That's right. And the more rejection you get, the more proof we both have that you're taking action.

"Besides, every rejection gives us new information. Sure, maybe a rejection means you still have more to learn about your market. But it also means there is plenty of room to grow.

"They'll come around. They always do."

She wasn't buying it. "How can you be so sure?"

This time I cracked a smile. "Well, I got a couple of Google Alerts on your name since we last spoke. It looked like a couple of your other articles went live. How did those fare?"

Heather explained how she woke up one morning to a few dozen new notifications on her social channels. At first, she couldn't figure out what was going on. Then she realized two of her articles had been published on the same day.

They earned her some new followers and generated engagement on social media. Plus, a few business coaches had let her know how useful her content was, and she had also answered a few questions from people interested in her ideas.

She'd even gotten a couple of leads in her inbox! Sadly for Heather, they were both tire-kickers who weren't that serious yet. They'd agreed to ask again if they ever needed more help, but they were both low-value opportunities, looking for do-it-yourself solutions.

 **Don't play to win all of them. Play to win the next one.**

Still, Heather admitted all the attention had given her a rush of satisfaction. She then let the cat out of the bag. "Brent, I need to tell you something. Before we started this whole process, I had a big opportunity that was put on hold. Not getting this deal was one of the main reasons I reached out to you. But I just got word that they are ready to move forward.

"I'm not sure how this will affect our work together. I mean, maybe I don't need all this after all. I'm still struggling to see how I could ever build a business just working with business coaches." I think Heather expected me to be shocked, but I had heard everything she was saying before—many times, from dozens of clients. I put down my coffee. "Heather, the last thing I want you to do is to stop running your agency. Of course, you have to meet the revenue needs and client obligations you have in front of you.

"If anything, landing this deal will relieve some of the desperation you're feeling and allow you to continue investing in this strategic work without the distracting pressure. Now, only you can make the decision about whether this is a process that you'd like to continue. We still have a long road ahead of us.

"But I do need you to commit to the process. If you're in, you need to be all in. I can't be convincing you of the merits of this process every time we meet.

"I don't need an answer today, but you need to take a look at your workload and determine if you'll still have time to work with me given this new client obligation. If that sounds good with you, I'd still like to talk about your voice, and about the third A in the 5-A Framework: Attract."

Heather agreed that she wanted to continue our session for today. This was great because, yes, Heather had been making progress with her articles. But they were still just good, not great. Her topics were on-point, but she wrote with a dry and overly professional voice, without her natural tone. And the stories she wrote about were, shall we say, less than engaging.

It's never fun to get rejected, but the truth is I could empathize with the publisher who turned her down. It just wasn't A+ material. So I opened my laptop to one of the articles Heather recently published.

"Your headline grabs attention. You've got that down, and it's working for you. Good job.

"But what happens next could use some work.

"Your 'Ultimate Guide' article, for instance, sometimes reads like a textbook. It's very academic and instructional. There is a ton of value, but we're not grabbing the reader's attention and getting them invested in reading. The article cuts right to the solution and isn't anchored in a story. And humans crave good stories."

I went on to explain how humans sat around campfires for tens of thousands of years. Stories were how we bonded—so today our brains are hardwired to connect through stories, not instructions. But then I got to the difficult stuff.

"Heather, do you mind if I give you some constructive feedback? I worry you might find it critical."

I could see her tense up, but she forced a smile. "Sure, of course. That's why I'm here, right?"

"I love working with you, Heather. You have a strong, fun personality. You're a firebrand. But so far, your articles read like they were written by the CEO of a large multinational corporation who's afraid of upsetting the apple cart. They're sterile. Risk-free. Kind of boring, if you'll forgive the word.

"I know the *real* Heather. She's passionate about her work, her clients, and her craft. So where is she? Why aren't you writing the same way you talk to me?"

Heather was quick with an answer. "Don't I need to write with a more professional voice? I need to seem bigger than I am. These kinds of clients won't do business with someone who's not already established."

Funnily enough, that was also something I'd heard a lot. "Heather," I replied, "what kind of clients do you want? The ones thinking they are going to be working with a large multinational corporate agency or the ones who are secretly wishing a firebrand like you would show them how to use the web? You don't just want leads; you want raving fans.

"You want people showing up at your doorstep who you've trained to think the way you think—and you want them ready to do business with you. You want them to have already gotten to know you as much as possible before that first conversation. So take off the restraints and be the real you!"

And just like that, something clicked—and Heather realized there was power in being herself. I showed her a couple of basic structures she could use to help her tell better stories with her articles. How to hook her audience within the first couple of sentences. How to create open loops that were only "closed" later. And how to build to a climax and give the reader a "payoff."

And I encouraged her to write as if she were talking to a potential client in person. I taught her that, while she still needed to write as a professional, she'd find it better to throw out what she learned about writing in high school and start making her own rules.

And then I paused. I wasn't sure if Heather was ready for one more assignment, but she seemed hungry for more. "Heather, there's also one more thing I'd like you to do. I need you to talk to enough coaches about their problems, pains, and struggles that you start to speak as if you are a business coach."

Heather thought for a moment. "Are you asking me to start a business coaching company?"

I laughed. "Not at all. Or at least not yet.

"And I know you're worried about extra work, but I need you to go talk to ten business coaches over the next two weeks. It's time for you to learn the art of customer development—so you can come to deeply understand your audience."

Heather was quite put off by this assignment. "Talking to ten people that I don't know in a week or two sounds like insanity."

"Fortunately for us both, Heather, you've been good at following the recipe so far; let's keep that positive momentum going."

Shortly after our meeting, I got an email from Heather that said, yes, she was committed to the process. This was great news— just as I thought she'd turn out to be, Heather was a quick study. She managed to find the time to talk to eight coaches and picked up a lot of cues about how coaches speak and think.

The next article she submitted for publishing was anchored in a compelling real-world story about working with Amy. She changed Amy's name for the article, of course, but she talked frankly about the root problem Amy had been facing.

Not only that, she unpacked what had been at stake when Amy had first come to her. She flexed her creative muscles a bit and painted the situation with vibrant detail.

Best of all, she wrote as if her customer avatar, Chris, was sitting right across from her. Heather threw out the multinational, corporate voice and wrote her article like she really talked—and how coaches talked. And she even kept a bit of her iconoclastic personality.

When she had finished, she wrote an email to the top publisher in her market. She felt so much more confident about the article that she was sure it would make the cut.

But then at the last second, she panicked. Instead, she emailed the article to one of the other publishers that had rejected her. A couple of days later, the publisher responded. "Now we're talking. We love this one!"

Heather had found her voice—and another success.

Chapter Eight Take Aways to Get Rich In The Deep End

♦ Each time you get rejected you have new information. You need to do better, be better, work harder to connect with what your market really cares about. Knowing what doesn't work is just as valuable as knowing what does work.

♦ Niching doesn't mean that we abandon our current clients. It doesn't mean we turn down all non-niche business. All it means is that you focus your limited marketing investments in a super focused way. You can still say yes to work outside your niche until you have enough momentum that "making the jump" to all-in as a market owner isn't a scary proposition, but a necessary step to grow.

♦ Pretending to be someone you're not is only going to attract the wrong people to your business. The more you are yourself, the more people you'll attract that are excited to work with who you are and how you operate.

♦ Write and speak in your content as if you're talking to one-person right in front of you. Don't become someone you're not.

CHAPTER NINE

The Third A—Attract

You likely have many problems in your business and life that you'd like to solve. Maybe even as quickly as possible. So what do you do?

Perhaps you search Google for those answers and discover a combination of organic webpage results and ads. Or pay more attention than you usually would to an ad on Facebook (an ad that targeted to you, of course) that talks about a problem you know too well. Maybe you don't actually know you have a problem until you hear someone talking about your symptoms on a podcast.

In all of those situations, the same thing happens. Your brain starts to consume the content with a single goal—relieving the pain or discomfort that it's experiencing.

Some of the messages you see will attract you to them. You'll have a hunch that the person doing the talking might be able to help. And some you'll instantly feel "aren't for you."

Here's the question: what *attracts* people to one message and not another? Can we reverse-engineer this attraction principle and leverage it for our own businesses—in a repeatable and proven manner?

Yes. When you master the third A of the 5-A Framework, you'll be able to attract customers to you whenever you want to.

Why Attract?

No matter the medium, the awareness activities you undertake must be strategically and tactically created with one purpose only: to attract ideal customers to your business. If you fail to do this, the time you spend on awareness will go to waste.

After all, you're not doing this for fun. There's only one reason to create *any* kind of awareness activity: to introduce your unique abilities to as much of your audience as you can.

Now, the bad news: publishing a piece of content on a blog, a stage, or another platform—doesn't automatically guarantee that you'll get any results. To keep things simple, I'm going to talk about content from now on. Because in one sense, any awareness activity you could focus on—from publishing a blog post, to appearing on a podcast, to creating a video, to speaking on a stage, or even launching an advertisement—is content.

Nearly 81% of the developed world is connected to the internet.[7] Chances are, if you're trying to reach someone, you can do it on the web. But all the other businesses and publishers in the world are competing with you for attention. By some estimates, nearly a trillion emails are sent every day.[8]

And that's just email. Never mind about social media posts and web pages and YouTube videos, and—let's stop for a second. I'm having a panic attack, and you probably are as well. But take heart, because there *is* good news.

Even with all of this information out there, humans are starving for *great* content. Collectively, our society adds about 25 quintillion bytes of data to the internet each day,[9] but most of that is what I call *throwaway content*. People read, watch, or listen to it—and "throw it away" by forgetting about it instantly.

This kind of content won't stand the test of time, but you have an opportunity to cut through the noise—to be a lighthouse in the storm. And you're going to do it by using your content to speak directly to the problems your market is facing—and showing you can solve those problems—*by telling stories*.

Storytelling and the art of narrative are baked into our cognitive structure. Yuval Noah Harari argues in his book *Sapiens* that, "Homo sapiens manage to [found] cities comprising tens of thousands of inhabitants and empires ruling hundreds of millions … [T]he secret was probably the appearance of fiction. Large numbers of strangers can cooperate successfully by believing in common myths."[10] It could be said that our species *dominated* this planet because we can make up stories—for example, about where to hunt with a minimum of interference from saber-toothed tigers.

This storytelling imperative also means we've evolved the ability to describe something that doesn't exist today. You can tell a customer about a feeling they're having right now, then paint a mental picture of a fictional future in which they don't have that feeling. Once they've eaten up every word of your story, you can invite them to work with you to make this vision a reality.

If your message resonates with a reader—and they believe you are a credible source of information—they will be attracted to you without even their conscious control. They will click, read, click, read, and click some more until they can get your solution to the tension that they're feeling.

Now, before you object, I promise you that you're talented enough. In fact, you can help *many* people solve the problems that are causing them stress, anxiety, and discomfort.

 **Talk about your ideal client's pain better than they understand it and they will instantly see you as an expert to solve their problems.**

Your problem *isn't* that you're unqualified. It's that your audience has no idea that you *are* qualified. That means it's your *job* to share with the world the amazing things you can do to solve their problems.

But without telling stories to tap into their deepest psyche, no one will ever show up at your door for your help. You owe it to them—and yourself—to create content that attracts.

Attract Leads with "Attracting" Content

To create the lasting material that is the opposite of throwaway content—whether blog articles, keynote speeches, social media content, or podcasts—pretend you're fishing.

There are four ingredients to content that attracts that are like different parts of your fishing setup. Just like you can change your lure or your line to make what you're doing more attractive to fish, you can experiment with these four ingredients—problems, worldviews, language, and voice—to make your content irresistible to your ideal customers.

Ingredient #1: Problems

Your audience has problems, and those problems are costing them a lot of money, time, and energy. You want to tell them you're the solution to those problems—that hiring you is easier and faster than solving those problems themselves.

Four Kinds of Problems.

In business, there are really only four main kinds of problems:

1. Money

2. Time

3. People

4. Passion

But you can't address them directly. You can't go to your audience and say, for example, "You're not making enough money! Hire me!"

First, this approach is tacky and lacks class. Second, "You're not making enough money" might be an underlying *core* issue, but that language probably doesn't reflect how your audience is thinking about their money problems.

Compare "You're not making enough money" to this statement: "You have a cash flow crisis—not because you don't have work but because your clients are failing to do what they need to on time, which is pushing your project schedule. That means you can't get paid, because your contract is based on deliverables, not dates. If this is something you're struggling with, schedule a strategy session and we'll map out how to change your billing terms."

I'm still talking there about a money problem, but I'm now discussing it in a way that people in my market can relate to. I'm "getting inside their head."

Never mind that their "cash flow crisis" is actually a symptom of an underlying, root problem with the way they bill, the terms in their contracts, or the systems they have set up to accept payments. They think they're having a cash flow crisis—so that's the language I need to use.

I can take this same core issue around money and put it through the lens of *time,* and I have yet another problem I can talk about that's relevant to my audience: "Creating invoices and chasing down clients is not a high-value task. Your time is more valuable than this. Consider delegating these ten-dollar-an-hour tasks to assistants so you can focus on growing your business!" Here's a look at the same issue through the other lenses:

People: "Finding the right people to take tasks of your plate can be a headache. It requires a lot of trust to let go of creating and sending invoices—collecting payments from clients—but without this person, you'll be stuck doing this monotonous admin task for the rest of your career, and that's no fun."

Passion: "I doubt sending invoices is your unique area of genius. Not only that, but it probably drains you. You might even needlessly delay doing this part of your business because it's such a pain, which of course causes cashflow problems and takes you away from doing what you're really meant to be focusing on: growing your business!"

By unpacking the same core issue, but through different lenses of money, time, people, and passion, I can zero in on highly relevant problems for my audience to sink their teeth into.

Five Stages of Awareness

That brings up an interesting point. Most people have mental blind spots. Your readers might intuitively know they have a problem but might be unaware of its true nature. Or they might not know at all. That's where you and your stories come in.

Your goal? Pretend every story is a miniature sales funnel and walk readers through five distinct psychological stages.

At first, they'll be *unaware*. They won't know about the problem they have, or they'll think they have a different problem than they actually do. You'll need to help them, then, discover their real problem. You'll make them *problem-aware*.

After that, you'll have to help them become *solution-aware*—so that they know a solution to their problem exists.

Now that they know they have a problem and that a solution exists, your next job is to make them *product-* or *service-aware*. Here you'll tell them that something you offer—and hopefully *only* you offer—can provide them the solution they now want.

Finally, thanks to your efforts, they'll be *ready to convert*. Now you can invite them to take you up on the next step in your sales process. (Buy, sign up, schedule a call, and so on.)

To make your audience feel you can solve your problem, every piece of content you create needs to walk them through these five stages.

Speaking to Customer Problems

Let's look more closely at the cash flow crisis I described above. If I were to let my imagination run wild, I could come up with a dozen or more problems and pain points just from this one issue:

- Lack of cash flow is keeping you from paying yourself.
- This rollercoaster of unpredictability makes it hard to hire new staff.
- Your staff might be concerned about their livelihood because you missed payroll once.
- Your clients have all the power and control over your income.
- You might be stuck using credit or debt to cover the gaps in project payments.
- You're tired of being in debt.
- Cash flow stress keeps you up at night.

- Being stressed about your business affects you personally.

- You might be working too hard to compensate for a billing issue.

- Income unpredictability affects your ability to do "normal" things, like get a mortgage.

- Your spouse or partner might view your business as risky.

- You're tired of chasing down clients for payments—it's not why you got into this business.

- You're starting to ask why you put up with all of this.

I understand these issues as an expert and authority within the market I serve. And talking about them in the content I create attracts ideal customers to my business. When you know your client's problem better than they do, that positions you as an expert.

Identify Problem. Describe Problem. Repeat.

You might worry you'll end up talking about the same problems over and over and over again, and that's okay. There's a lot of noise in the marketplace, and your customer probably won't hear you the first time—so you need to keep at it. But you certainly don't have to repeat yourself verbatim.

For example, I host a webinar just about every week. I've been running it for almost three years. And on that webinar, I talk about the three core problems my company solves—week in and week out.

The trick is, I do it from a hundred different angles. It seems fresh and new to my audience, but it's not. I'm just framing the material in new ways to help them hear my message.

And it continues to work. Some people show up five and six times before they finally buy—but they definitely *do* buy.

How to Find Customer Problems

To come up with all those different angles, I start with actual problems people have told me about. I think of recent conversations I've had. I refer to emails I've received from customers or prospects. And—the best way—I speak directly to people in my market.

You can do the same with informal conversations, formal interviews, or surveys.

Informal Conversations. An informal conversation is one without a predefined script or set of interview questions to guide it.

Most service professionals do this naturally. After all, these kinds of conversations tend to happen at conferences, meetups, or on phone calls.

Informal conversations are valuable because they force both you and the person you're talking with to think about problems. You can ask questions like: "What's keeping you up at night right now?" Then you can follow up with open-ended prompts: "Tell me more." "Why is that?"

Since these conversations often happen in the ordinary course of business, I recommend using a notepad or an Evernote-style software program to capture problems, pain points, or symptoms that your prospective clients run into. (You never know when you'll hear the idea that will help you frame your services better!)

I keep a spreadsheet of headline and topic ideas. I also sometimes email myself subject lines to store for later use.

One of my clients, Nate, records a short (and very rough) video for his content team to write articles from directly after sales calls. These videos are often only seven or eight minutes and provide enough context around a problem to write a 1,500-word article.

Formal Interviews. Few service professionals have formal interviews with their current and prospective customers. That's a shame because it's the best technique I've found to learn about new markets, then translate that information into product and service offerings.

Formal interviews—often called customer development interviews or CDIs—allow you to systematically interview customers in your market to validate hypotheses about problems, solutions, and productized service models.

Formal interviews can consist of a list of questions or can be delivered as a story script to help you understand your customers. You can download sample scripts in the Get Rich In The Deep End Field Guide at OwnYourMarket.com/Guide.

One note: when conducting formal CDIs, you typically want to engage in one to two dozen interviews over a couple of weeks so you can really saturate yourself in your market. This immersive approach is the easiest way to get a rich set of qualitative data on your audience. My personal record is seventy-eight interviews in one week. Not recommended.

Surveys. While my preference is to always begin with interviews, surveys can also be a useful way to get a wide-ranging idea of the surface-level problems that exist within your market. (That is, assuming you have access to some kind of list.)

Unfortunately, you can never be too sure that a respondent wasn't distracted when they answered. You also don't have the opportunity to read body language or tone-of-voice or ask open-ended follow-up questions that might uncover insights around more significant issues.

Still, you may decide to use surveys. If so, I highly recommend keeping the survey itself relatively short—one or two questions, if possible—to ensure that you get as much engagement as you can. If you need to ask more than "What's the #1 problem about X keeping you up at night?"—where X, of course, is your main service or problem area—then I recommend interviews.

Ingredient #2: Worldviews

Customers in your market also share particular perspectives on "how things are." These worldviews might be shared by your entire market, or they may be beliefs that are only held by certain customer groups or avatars.

As an example, here are some competing worldviews about WordPress within the web professional market:

- WordPress is a gift from the heavens vs. WordPress is "evil."
- WordPress is for beginners vs. WordPress shouldn't be touched by beginners.
- WordPress is a security nightmare vs. WordPress, in the right hands, is secure and safe.

To different people in the market I serve, each of these statements is "true." By understanding these worldviews, I can create content, products, and services that speak to these viewpoints.

My popular article, "Never Say WordPress When Selling a Web Design Project," struck a chord because the issue was so polarizing.[11]

Some people love WordPress so much that when they saw that headline, they freaked out and were ready to pounce on me. What they found when they read the article was a compelling argument about why you shouldn't discuss technology early on in the sales process. I talked about my personal journey learning this fact, and my experience was hard to argue with.

But the WordPress haters *also* clicked. They were ready to bring their metaphorical pitchforks and torches, like the real ones the villagers had in the old *Frankenstein* movie—only to find that I had made a compelling argument that was different from what *they* expected. Instead, they learned about sales, and they had to put their rage away.

Understanding Your Customers' Worldviews

If you don't work to understand your market's worldview, you'll be taking a chance on whether you'll be able to attract them. But *with* this understanding, you can intentionally play to:

- Beliefs
- Biases
- Opinions
- Stereotypes
- Workflows
- Lifestyles
- Habits
- Routines, and more

You might not have considered the different vantage points that various parts of your audience have. But by speaking fluently about the different worldviews within your market, you'll help your audience feel comfortable engaging with you—and ensure that there are fewer barriers to attracting them.

As you get to know your market more, listen for worldviews. Catalog them. Write them down and explore them as traits of your customer avatar. And when you get a chance to talk to customers, ask questions like this:

- "Tell me about a typical day for you."
- "Walk me through your workflow for doing _____."
- "What are your goals? What are you working toward?"
- "If you could wave a magic wand, what would work look like for you?"
- "What obstacle or trouble do you and others in this market share?"

You might even try a creative exercise I enjoy doing from time to time—writing a journal entry as if I'm my ideal customer. This might seem strange, but trust me, it can help you see the *real* world your customer lives in.

This is helpful, because you may be under the impression that your clients are just sitting around thinking about you *all day*.

But they're not. Your clients are wrestling with their businesses, changing poopy diapers, arguing at home, and wondering how they're going to pay the bills—just like the rest of us. So the more you can do to get in their heads, the better.

For example, I know many of my clients struggle to get all of their work done by 5 p.m. They usually have piles of unread emails or undone to-dos. I know that this issue hurts their personal lives because they carry their work into their personal lives following their workday. They continue to check their phones and feel guilty for not getting their inbox to zero.

This issue is a significant problem, which keeps my clients from living the life they really want. Just reading about it now probably has you nodding in frustration. *That's the power of content that attracts.*

But by identifying that worldview in my market, I can help my clients understand more about themselves. They can't see their own lives because they're too close to them, but when they see their lives reflected in what I'm saying, they recognize themselves.

And there is a lot of power in that kind of understanding.

Ingredient #3: Language

Besides understanding your audience's problems and worldviews, you also need to learn how to speak their language. Every market has specific words, phrases, and acronyms they use to talk about their work. By using the terminology your audience is familiar with, you can quickly establish credibility.

For example, web professionals have their fair share: CMS, HTML, SEO, and so on. If you were speaking to a website designer, you could—and should—use those terms generously. However, you'd probably want to avoid them at your family's next Thanksgiving dinner. Unless, of course, you live in a family of designers.

"Talking the talk" attracts people to you. It says that you know your stuff and can help them solve their unique problems. Understanding their language lets you participate in the conversations that happen in your market. Using that language says you belong.

That's important. You have to belong to lead. Think of Amy's friend Jake back at the beginning of this book: he knew the words and phrases used by the restaurateurs he was targeting. He even made a joke of the fact that he was an outsider—a joke that, paradoxically, drew people even closer to him.

Here's what happens when you *don't* do that. I once spoke about the business of digital agencies at a printing conference. It was a giant convention full of folks in a declining industry who were desperate to learn about what to do in the future.

I knew nothing about the industry and didn't know their language. I spoke *my* language—and their eyes glassed over. As a result, my talk bombed. I was too concerned about telling them how to compete against the big commodity DIY website services when I should have started with "Here's what a website is."

Where to Find Customer Language

If you have some experience in the market you are targeting— for example, you used to be in it, or you work closely with a few clients in the space—using your audience's language can be a great advantage.

If you're brand new, however, you'll need to work on learning the words your audience uses. One misplaced phrase and you could kill the belief that you know what you're talking about.

For example, if I were to say, "SEO helps websites look better on mobile phones," my audience would likely cringe a little. ("What is this guy talking about? SEO is about getting found in the search engines. Did he mean 'responsive design'? Does he even have a clue?")

When learning your audience's language, be on the lookout for:

- Terms (responsive design)
- Phrases (hire slow, fire fast)
- Acronyms (HTML, CSS, SEO)
- Tone (friendly, funny, brash)
- Inside jokes (PITA client)

The best way to learn insider language is in one-on-one interviews with customers, prospects, influencers, or champions (influential customers who are willing to go to bat for you in your new market).

But really—*any* time you are speaking with someone in your market, take the time to slow down the conversation when they say something you don't understand. Simple questions help, like: "Can you tell me a little more about what that phrase means to you?"

Remember, the more people you speak with in your market, the sooner you'll master your audience's language. Personally, when I first get into a market, I might schedule thirty to fifty or more customer-development interviews *per week*. This requires a lot of time and energy, but it helps me quickly master my audience's language—and that knowledge is invaluable when I'm creating content, talks, and sales offers.

Even today, after being in the digital agency market for two decades, I'm still learning new words and phrases. The industry is always evolving and changing. I have to keep up with the trends to stay relevant in my industry—and so will you.

Ingredient #4: Voice

If there is specific *language* that people use in an industry, it makes sense that there are also styles of *talking* that work well for one audience or another. As well as styles of talking that *don't* work. The style of talking you adopt for your market is called your *voice*.

I have discovered my voice by practicing—a lot. You don't find it *before* you begin to write or speak; you find it *through* writing and speaking.

If you aren't sure what your authentic voice is yet, don't worry. Just keep working at it. If you're struggling, imagine you're talking to just one person—your ideal client—over coffee. You're comfortable and engaged, and just being *you*.

The closer your published content gets to this kind of voice, the more people in your market will become attracted to working with you. Keep in mind, though, that your voice will often be shaped by what's appropriate for your audience.

Could you imagine noted entrepreneur Gary Vaynerchuk talking the way he does to an audience of librarians? Dropping f-bombs and swinging his brash, over-the-top personality around?

No, me neither. Vaynerchuk's personality "works" in the world of entrepreneurship because we value his unusual style. Many entrepreneurs grew up breaking all the rules, so it makes sense for him to adopt the voice of a rule-breaker. But for a group of people who are stereotypically quiet, orderly, and organized—like librarians—Vaynerchuk's voice is simply the *wrong* fit.

On the one hand, your voice should be as unique to you as your personality. It's what will help you when you write articles and blog posts, when you are interviewed on podcasts, and when you take the stage to speak. On the other hand, your voice needs to avoid *driving away* your audience. You need to fit in with your market. It's a balancing act

Now, I'm certainly not encouraging you to say, "Damn the torpedoes" and speak like Gary V. But you can look at *how* Vaynerchuk speaks and get some good tips—four, in fact—about how to shape a voice of your own.

Tip #1: Stand for Something

Take a position. If something isn't right and it makes you mad, call it out. I'm not saying you should complain or whine, but if you have strongly held beliefs about how your area of expertise *should* work, become an evangelist for that way of thinking. Advocate and defend your position.

For example, I have a deep dislike for rotating homepage sliders on agency websites. I think they display a lack of conviction about what a company wants to say on the homepage.

Now, there's a chance you have a rotating slider. Maybe you don't. But hearing me talk about them might make you feel *something*—good or bad—and there's nothing wrong with that.

If I can state my position and sway you to my way of thinking on this one issue, there's a better chance I can attract your attention long enough to convince you to engage with me in a deeper relationship. And that's what I *really* want.

Tip #2: Be Contrarian

Not everyone feels the same way about popular ideas, concepts, or trends. If you consider the size of a typical market—with thousands or even hundreds of thousands of potential clients—you'll almost always find a percentage who don't agree with the conventional position.

You can take advantage of this fact to make your content and message stand out. If everyone is publishing ideas that reflect the majority opinion—and no one is representing the minority—you'll attract more attention by stating the contrary opinion. And you'll have a better chance of getting *all* of the minority on your side (rather than just a small percentage of the majority).

For example, let's look again at my "Never Say WordPress" article. At the time I published it, most of the web community was worshiping WordPress. People felt passionate about the platform and its potential, but because WordPress was free, clients started devaluing the entire industry—expecting web development to cost a lot less than it does. So WordPress had a lot of detractors, too.

When I published an article titled, "Never Say WordPress When Selling a Web Design Project," the web community exploded. The minority who hated WordPress had abandoned it because "mainstream" content was so pro-WordPress. They were also typically experiencing deep dissatisfaction with their own business *because* of WordPress. So when I said, "Let's stop talking about it," it instantly attracted them to me.

The article reached the "most popular" position on a major influencer site. It generated instant credibility for our brand and thousands of email signups for our list. I got more fan mail than I had ever received in my life. (Yes, I also got more hate mail from the majority!)

That's the power of holding a contrarian view to attract the minority, not just the majority, of a market.

However, being a contrarian doesn't mean simply complaining. Even though you are presenting a less popular counterpoint to the mainstream opinion, remember to keep things positive.

Tip #3: Remember That Professionalism Is Subjective

When I first started my business, I believed I was supposed to communicate a certain way. Most of the style I developed was based on how the big companies did it.

The problem, of course, is that these companies were not *my* company. Emulating the way they spoke put me at a disadvantage. Instead of relying on my unique abilities and my small size, I tried to compete head-to-head with the goliaths.

I tried to hide the fact that we were two guys living in a loft in downtown Denver, building websites and apps from home. I would insert a lot of extraneous garbage into the content we wrote about our business to make us seem much bigger than we were.

I validated this behavior under the guise of "professionalism." I wanted to show up as a professional in the web design and digital marketing space. I wanted small businesses to think we were a "real" business.

Unfortunately, we would attract people who wanted to work with a bigger company. Eventually, they would figure out that we weren't—and we risked buyer's remorse.

I understand now that we could have communicated professionally without having to act like we were something we weren't. Most markets are big enough that you can attract ideal clients by simply being who you are, even if you're small.

Here's the kind of language we used: "Our leadership team has been developing web applications for over two decades combined. We have a global team of talent that can help build your online business."

And here's the kind of thing we should have said: "We're two young and hungry guys that can't wait to write code to help your business grow. We're in such demand that we searched the globe and found two more people in Poland—and they just might be the most talented developers in the world."

Which of those descriptions stands out to you? One attempts to hide the smallness; the other leans into it and turns it into the reason the agency is unique.

Larger companies need to appeal to a mass audience because they need so many customers just to survive. As a smaller shop, you don't have to attract everyone—just a few of the right customers.

Tip #4: Don't Worry About Making Everyone Happy

Now, by communicating your unique market position, you'll likely repel people who aren't right for you. That's something you need to be okay with. In fact, people deciding that they *don't* want to work with you could be taken as an indicator that you're doing things right. You don't want to repel the "good fit" clients, of course, but neither do you want to waste your time with clients who aren't right for you.

Always remember what you're trying to accomplish. If you publish an article to an audience of a thousand people on a blog, it's okay if almost all of them dislike your material.

You don't need a thousand clients tomorrow; you need one or two. If what you say turns away a big chunk of an audience—but you've published what you think the *right person needs to hear*—then do your best to shrug off the negative criticism.

Tip #5: Keep It Positive and Relevant

Do your best to avoid complaining or being negative in your content. The purpose of the content you produce is to inspire your audience into taking action and investing in your services. Even when you are identifying problems and issues your audience might be experiencing, you want to frame the situation as an opportunity for change.

Focus on what matters to your audience and the issues they're trying to overcome. Likely your stance on politics, religion, and other controversial topics aren't highly relevant to the business services and solutions you offer to solve real market problems.

I've watched many agency owners publish great content to attract leads and clients, only to fill their social media pages with non-relevant rants about politics or highly polarizing social issues that likely deters ideal clients from ever contacting them.

Keep your content relevant to your target audience and stay positive as best you can.

Create Your Content Using the Three-Act Structure

As I mentioned above, humans are a narrative species.

Tens of thousands of years by the campfire. Months- or years-long migrations on foot. Countless pieces of tradition and culture handed down from generation to generation. These have hardwired our brains for a love of stories.

Intuitively, we know that every story needs a beginning, middle, and end. When we hear a story that forgets one of those elements, we're left thinking, "Is that all there is?"

But Steven Pressfield, in his book *Nobody Wants to Read Your Sh*t: Why That Is and What You Can Do About It*, says even a beginning, middle, and end aren't enough.[12] He says every story should also follow a three-act structure, just like a play:

1. Hook your audience in Act One.

2. Build tension and complications in Act Two.

3. Then resolve everything with a payoff in Act Three.

Hook, build, payoff—it's that simple. Sure, you can get fancier. There are seemingly limitless elements to storytelling: concept, theme, narrative arc, inciting action, and many more. But if you miss those three essential elements, you simply don't have a story, and your reader will know it. They'll stop paying attention—and they likely won't even understand why. The truth is that there was simply no story to compel them to pay attention.

Now, maybe you're thinking "I'm just trying to write blog posts for my business, not tell stories! My content about Facebook advertising isn't a three-act play." But it is.

Here's an example: I couldn't figure out how to get clients for my business. I tried everything. When all hope was lost, I spent $250,000 on Facebook Ads.

I learned about writing ad copy, A/B testing, and marketing funnels. This investment got me an unofficial MBA in online advertising.

I scaled beyond seven figures in record time. I signed up thousands of new customers. I solved the "get more clients" problem.

And I turned my business around.

- *Act One: The Hook.* "I lost $250,000."

- *Act Two: The Build.* "I learned about all kinds of things and grew in no time flat."

- *Act Three: The Payoff.* "I saved my company."

See how easy that was? The three-act structure works in articles, blog posts, keynotes, landing pages, ads, and even marketing emails and outbound call scripts.

Three Acts in Action

I have a basic framework for articles that helps me write authority content designed to attract and convert the right readers into leads and clients. You'll notice right away that it incorporates the three-act structure:

1. *Hook*

    a. Establish credibility.

    b. Identify the problem(s).

2. *Build*

    c. Unpack the problem by telling a story, anecdote, case study, quote, or example.

    d. Walk through the solution, step by step.

3. *Payoff*

    e. Explain the net benefit (what is the result?).

    f. End with a clear call to action.

Now, don't confuse this framework for a formula. Formulas say that if you follow them, you'll get the same result every time. This is *not* a formula. It's a framework because it provides you a box to operate in so you can start creating content—instead of being overwhelmed by "I can't write," or "I don't know where to start."

Here, once again, is "Never Say WordPress." I used the framework to write this piece. As you read, see if you can find the elements in action:[13]

Before selling my web agency, HotPress Web, last year and starting UGURUS, a new venture to help web professionals become more profitable, I pitched a lot of website projects.

My proposal folder has over 950 bids in it. Of course, I didn't win all of these, but I did close several million dollars in website deals over my tenure. Our typical project was in the ballpark of $20,000. When I started out, I had a hard time winning $3,000 deals.

Until I learned how to sell and build value, I wasn't getting paid enough. Sometimes it would take everything I could muster to win a project for $1,200, and I would end up promising $3,000 in services.

I was also spending a lot of time pitching business that never panned out. I had a hard time winning 1 in 10 bids. The time suck was draining away my hours to be productive outside of pitching business—like actually getting project work done.

I was frustrated. I began looking for answers.

The Status Quo

The typical process for me looked something like this:

A prospect calls me asking for website services.

I ask what they need, a little info about their business, and what kind of features and functionality they are thinking about.

I demo what we can do (show the technology of the hour: WordPress, Drupal, Shopify, BigCommerce, LightCMS, Business Catalyst, etc.)

I deep dive into the different functionality they need on their project and show them how it can be done.

I send a proposal.

I start following up.

Inevitably I would get into some follow-up conversations with the prospective customer about my platform of choice. Every time we would spend countless hours deep diving into the technology.

"Can it do this? What about...?"

Eventually, the customer would tell me that the other company bidding on the project is using a different technology, usually something similar to what I was pushing.

Then it would happen: the technology debate.

Is WordPress better than Drupal?

Is Opensource better than Software as a Service?

Who has control over the site?

How is it backed up?

Where will it be hosted?

The worst part about it was that most of this software we were debating was free and open. There was no cost associated with the platform. We were spending all of this energy discussing something that really had no bearing on my expertise and the value I brought to the table.

Before I knew it, the customer was choosing between software platforms and not which company was going to provide the best solution.

As WordPress became more popular, it got worse. The technology debate softened, but then all of my competition was offering the same technology solution that I was. I lost differentiation.

An Epiphany

As I sold more projects, worked with more businesses, visited more offices, I started to see patterns. I began thinking about what I was really doing.

Was web design just that? Designing web pages and loading content? Was it programming and open source and PHP this and .NET that? Or were we doing something much bigger for our customers? I always assumed that when a customer called me for a website, that the problem they are trying to solve was getting a new website, but it's not.

Businesses are looking to solve sales, marketing, logistics, customer service, or public relations problems. Websites just happen to be a great solution to problems in those areas (and many others).

Zap! (Lightning strike.)

When business owners call and ask about getting a website, they are trying to solve an issue that goes beyond their request for some design and HTML. They couldn't actually care less about what platform you use. No matter how great WordPress is.

The #1 Problem

So I changed my approach. At first, it was subtle adjustments. I started listening more intently. I asked a lot of questions to try to get to the root problem that the customer faced in their business.

Let me provide some examples:

Old Approach. Customer: "We need to be able to update the content on our website." Me: "Content management is what WordPress is all about." Outcome: Sell a WordPress solution and compete with everyone else doing the same thing.

New Approach. Customer: "We need to be able to update the content on our website." Me: "What kind of content do you plan on updating?" Customer: "Our products change quarterly. We also want to blog." Me: "Why do your products change quarterly? And who is responsible for blogging?" Customer: "That is when our catalog gets updated. We haven't thought about who will blog, we just know we need one."

Me: "Is it necessary for anyone to be aware of your catalog being updated, or do you just need the content changed? And besides knowing you need a blog, what is the problem that needs solving?" Customer: "Yes! We'd love our customers to get an email for a promotion each time our catalog is updated. We'd like to attract more customers through our blog—you know, let people know what we are up to."

Outcome: Eventually create a compelling solution for a dynamic website project, content management training, ghostwriter with an SEO strategy for blog content, email marketing template creation, email marketing training, and some custom content development.

Instead of taking my prospect's "stated needs" as absolute, I question all of them. Eventually, they will fess up to the real problem they are most likely trying to solve—getting more customers.

The more I practiced this technique, the higher priced my proposals got and the more I won. My clients ate it up. No one else I was competing against talked like this. Everyone sold to the technology.

The Challenge

So I started to give myself challenges. I would see how long I could go with a client without ever mentioning the technology we planned to build on.

First, it was a meeting. Then two. By the time I sold my agency, on most deals, I would go through seven or eight interactions in the sales cycle without ever talking about a lick of technology.

If you are having a hard time building value for your website services, then I have a challenge for you: stop selling the technology. See how long you can go without mentioning WordPress, Drupal, Joomla, Shopify, or whatever your technology poison is.

Can you identify the different parts of the framework? First, I established my credibility by talking about my history in business, then identified the problem—follow-up hell. Then I told my story and walked through my new way of approaching things. Finally, I explained the result—less competition—and ended by telling my readers what to do next.

How to Use the Framework

If you find yourself stuck on content, first look at the problems your audience has and the solutions you provide. Create your headline or high-level concept, then use the 1-2-3 framework.

Write a sentence about why you're a credible person to talk about this problem. Then write one about what the problem is. Think of a story or anecdote where you or a client experienced this problem. By that point, you should be well on your way to a finished piece of content.

When you're done, check back over the content to make sure you're following the Hook, Build, Payoff structure. Did you reward the reader and resolve the tension at the end? Did you tell them what you wanted them to do?

If you're still stuck, you can find a fill-in-the-blanks worksheet in the OYM Field Guide at OwnYourMarket.com/Guide.

Using the Framework with Other Forms of Content

I like blog posts and guest publishing for many reasons:

- You can write from anywhere.
- Writing lives on the web for eternity (most of the time).
- You can edit and rewrite for clarity and polish.
- The written word can be very clear.
- Search engines love written content (Google can drive a lot of eyeballs).
- Most markets have a lot of established publishers with huge audiences.
- You can repurpose written content later into other mediums.
- Blog posts can go viral, and there's no limit to the number of eyeballs if it's compelling content.

But there are lots of other ways to get your message in front of your audience:

1. Write articles for print.
2. Write micro-posts for Facebook or Twitter.
3. Record videos for YouTube.
4. Broadcast live on Facebook, Instagram, and so on.
5. Write bots for Messenger.

6. Guest on a podcast.

7. Host a podcast.

8. Launch a daily vlog.

9. Guest on a webinar.

10. Host your own webinar.

11. Give a toast at a local meetup group.

12. Deliver a keynote at a conference.

13. Write and broadcast emails to your list.

14. Write ads for Facebook, Google, etc.

Intimidating, isn't it? There's *no way* I could figure out how to create content for all of these platforms. Maybe you feel the same way.

But although each of these platforms has its own nuances and tactics, what it takes to tell a story remains the same: Hook. Build. Payoff. That's all.

Let's pretend, for example, you have to come up with a talk for an industry stage. You'll see the process for creating that speech looks very similar to what you'd do for a guest post:

1. Write one sentence about what you want your audience to understand by the end of your talk.

2. Create an outline with that sentence at the top and a section for your Hook, Build, and Payoff.

3. Write out bullet points for each.

4. Unpack the content based on the time allotted. If it's a five-minute talk, then you'd better be concise. If you have a ninety-minute keynote, you can probably create some mini Hook, Build, Payoff loops within the overarching three-act structure.

5. Add a compelling call-to-action for your audience to follow up with you. Offer a juicy resource, free audit, consultation, or some other value-add that people would gladly pay money for.

6. Practice your talk at least once from start to finish. Bonus points if you do your talk in front of a live test audience to see if your story works.

When presented with a new content medium, you'll have to learn the mechanics, but one thing will remain the same: you can replicate the power of the campfire and tap into thousands of years of human sociology with Steven Pressfield's simple Hook, Build, Payoff structure.

Combine this with the insights you've learned from customer interviews around problems, workflows, and worldviews; the depth and texture you've added to your content with your voice; and the specific language you've mastered from your market, and you have created content that will surely *attract* your audience to your agency.

Chapter Nine Take Aways to Get Rich In The Deep End

◆ People are constantly seeking solutions to their most pressing problems. Whether on Google or scanning headlines. Speak to the problems.

◆ Attract ideal clients by talking about stuff they care about: i.e. their problems, not your solution.

◆ People crave stories. Tell your audience about people just like them that had the same problems and how you helped them overcome the challenges.

◆ When you communicate about a core problem in your market—like making more money—make sure to do so from the lens and worldview of your market. Talk about this problem in a *context* that they will understand and connect with.

◆ The better you can explain why a problem exists in your market, the more people you'll attract that have this problem.

◆ There's a lot of noise in the marketplace, and your customer probably won't hear you the first time—so you need to keep at it.

◆ Worldviews can be powerful lenses to creating more content around the same idea. Use beliefs, biases, opinions, stereotypes, workflows, lifestyles, habits, and routines as different vantage points to cover the same idea.

◆ Write a "day in the life of" for your client. If your client had a diary, what would the entry for today say? Knowing this will help you create content that more deeply connects and resonates with your market.

◆ Master your market's language. The phrases, acronyms, and slogans that are commonly used. Adopting this language says that you're part of the club. It gives indicators that people should trust you.

◆ You don't find your *voice* before you write or speak–you find it *by* writing and speaking. So, if you're waiting to get clear on this before you start, you'll be waiting a long, long time.

◆ Your voice is a unique fingerprint that makes you unique in your market. It's a way to stand out by just being yourself and speaking to your market as the best version of yourself and your agency.

◆ I have a simple mantra with content and social engagement: make it better.

◆ Keep your content relevant to your target audience and stay positive as best you can.

CHAPTER TEN

Heather Builds Authority

Heather looked at me with frustration and disappointment. "Brent, I think I should choose another niche. I don't think business coaches are the right fit for me."

"And why is that?"

Heather sighed. "They don't trust me because I don't have enough experience. So far, I've only worked with Amy. We did a great job for her, but I can't just give a single example when prospective clients ask me who I've worked with."

 **Pretending to be someone you're not is only going to attract the wrong people to your business.**

Heather went on to tell me what prompted her self-doubt. Just a few days earlier, a coach had called her after reading her "Ultimate Guide" and asked her about her experience with business coaches.

She was taken off guard and told the prospective client that Amy was her only account so far. Then her lead made a snarky comment about how her article made it seem that she had a lot more experience—and maybe she wasn't a good fit after all.

Heather went on, panic creeping into her voice. "I just kind of picked business coaches randomly in one of our first meetings together. Shouldn't I pick something else? Another market that maybe I have more experience in? Jake's doing restaurants. Perhaps those are a better fit—he seems to be succeeding despite his inexperience when he started. I don't know Brent. I just feel like I'll never get the momentum I need."

I could see that Heather was experiencing the same crisis of confidence that everyone goes through when they begin to master anything. I carry a copy of Seth Godin's best-selling book, The Dip, with me just for these occasions.[14]

I pulled it out and read one of my favorite sections to Heather:

At the beginning, when you first start something, it's fun. You could be taking up golf or acupuncture or piloting a plane or doing chemistry—doesn't matter; it's interesting, and you get plenty of good feedback from the people around you. Over the next few days and weeks, the rapid learning you experience keeps you going. Whatever your new thing is, it's easy to stay engaged in it. And then the Dip happens. The Dip is the long slog between starting and mastery. A long slog that's actually a shortcut because it gets you where you want to go faster than any other path.

Heather looked at me with a sheepish smile. "So I'm in the Dip? You're saying the new and shiny has worn off."

"Yep."

"And if I start over with a new market, it will be new and exciting again. But then I'll experience the Dip all over again?"

"Unfortunately, yes."

"How long is the Dip when focusing on a new market? If I'm going to do this work, I need to know. Are we talking about a few weeks here—or a few years?"

I could sense a new level of tension in Heather's voice. "Heather, I hate to break it to you, but I don't have that kind of crystal ball. Business coaches are a big market.

"What's important is that you keep doing what you're doing. A few months ago, you had never been published in any market. And there weren't any business coaches besides Amy who knew who you were.

"Now you're published, with more articles on the way. You have strangers calling, emailing, and signing up for your newsletter.

"That's progress. And unless there's some glaring issue you're not telling me about, I recommend that you keep going since you're getting results. Some nasty comment from a single bad-fit lead doesn't mean you should toss your strategy."

Heather thought for a moment. "I guess you're right. One comment isn't a good reason to change direction. But what can I do to help build more trust and do a better job answering that question next time?"

I explained to Heather what one of my own sales mentors, Townsend Wardlaw, had passed on to me. "There are two processes that buyers go through when they make a purchase: they try to measure benefits and they try to mitigate risk.

"Yes, your prospects need to understand the value they will get by working with you. But they also need to know that investing in your services is safe. When someone asks about your past experience, they are trying to assess how risky an investment you are.

"So the next time someone asks you about your experience helping business coaches, instead of answering that question, what I want you to do is pretend they're asking this question instead: 'What proof can you give me that my investment with you will be safe?'"

I could see Heather processing this information.

 **There are three types of results you can provide: tangible, quantifiable, and emotional.**

"Well, I've been working with all kinds of businesses for the last ten years. I would probably start by talking about the problems that Amy had before we started working with her, and the results we helped her achieve. I would then talk about some of our best examples of building online businesses for clients that were similar to coaches."

This was what I wanted to hear. "You're starting to get the hang of this, Heather. What I'd like to do next is give you a framework that will help you answer these questions with facts that will help mitigate the risk your prospective clients might be feeling.

"Remember our fourth A, authority?"

Heather did. "Yes, like the before and after image that I included in my blog post?"

"You got it, Heather. That's an example of authority. It says, 'I've done this before, and I get results.' And that's the basis for building your authority.

"But we need to help you go further than that. The more we can establish you as an authority for this market, the more your prospects will trust you. The less risk they'll see when they consider working with you, and the faster they'll buy.

"Most businesses are the same. Maybe 5% of issues differ from industry to industry, but the other 95% is common to them all. And you have a lot of experience working with all sorts of businesses and organizations, right?"

Heather nodded. "I've been doing this with my agency for over ten years. And I worked in corporate marketing before that."

I couldn't help but smile. "So you already are an authority. We just need to position your experience in a way that builds credibility with business coaches. I think it's time to unpack your proof points."

I pulled out a worksheet with a few columns for different proof points—facts and figures that build trust and credibility—and I prompted Heather to start filling them in.

At first, I could see her struggling to talk about her accomplishments and accolades. But by the end of the exercise, Heather had listed two dozen selling points that spoke to why she could be trusted to solve the issues her market faced.

Most of the points were numbers-based and helped quantify the benefit she had delivered to businesses of all types over the last decade. A couple came from an experience she had gleaned working with coaches. They all painted a compelling picture of why she could be trusted to help her clients grow their businesses.

"These are looking really good, Heather. Take a look."

It was Heather who was smiling now. "Apparently, I've done a lot more that could help business coaches than I thought."

I nodded. "And now you have a tool that can be used as a reference when it's time to write articles, update your website, talk to prospects, or take the stage at conferences. So now I want you to put these proof points to work on your website's "About" page and your social media profiles.

"You don't need to overdo it, but each piece of content you write and have out there on the web should have three to five proof points woven throughout. Is that something that you can do?"

"Easy enough, Brent.

"And to tell you the truth, I can't wait to get started."

Chapter Ten Take Aways to Get Rich In The Deep End

◆ The biggest test to owning your market is whether or not you'll be able to stick with things when they become boring and repetitive. On the other side of this is excitement, momentum, and scale.

◆ Progress, not perfection.

◆ Tell your prospects why they should trust you. What results have you gotten people like them? What proof can you show?

◆ The first person that you need to convince that you're an authority is yourself. Believe you're an expert and your market will follow.

◆ There are three types of results you can provide: tangible, quantifiable, and emotional.

CHAPTER ELEVEN

The Fourth A—Authority

If you've been in business for any length of time, you've probably had a warm referral to an ideal client. You know *how* that happens. Someone vouches for you and introduces a prospective client. When you reach out, the lead already has respect for you.

But have you ever thought about *why* they have that respect? Because they already have respect for your mutual friend, as well as an existing relationship with them. And that mutual friend has suggested you can solve the lead's problem, so they're willing to talk to you.

You have, as the dictionary defines it, "the power to influence others, especially because of one's commanding manner or one's recognized knowledge about something."[15]

You have *authority*—the fourth A.

Immediately, your referred potential client wants your guidance. They let you take the lead, and they already trust you—you didn't have to do anything.

This is what being an authority brings you:

- High trust from day one because you're viewed as "the expert."

- Lower friction during the sales process.
- A position as the *only* option the client initially wants to work with.
- Less price sensitivity to your services.

Now think about what would happen if *many* people thought you were an authority. Your market would talk about you. You'd get third-party endorsements. It would become far easier to get booked for speaking engagements or land guest posts on trusted platforms. Your case studies and proof points would then have an extra air of validity.

When you're an authority at scale, the benefits multiply.

 **You've already lost if you have to explain to someone how they fit in your world.**

Why Authority-Motivated Leads Are Better

When it comes to referrals and word of mouth, you have a pre-existing source of authority: the advocate who referred you.

The person referring you does the hard work for you. They hype you up, they vouch for you, and they put their own credibility on the line when they introduce you to a prospective lead.

But if you take them out of the equation, you end up with the kind of lead that randomly finds you from a Google search, spends roughly eight seconds scanning your website, and then fills out your contact form. (And they have probably done the same with a dozen other companies just like yours.)

Here's the big problem: when random leads show up, they think *they* are the authority and that you're "just one more vendor."

Those leads don't know anything about your deep experience serving their market or the results you've provided many businesses like theirs.

These leads are "cold"—as opposed to those referred to you, which are "warm." And with cold leads, you start at square one—every time.

Exhibit 7

It probably makes sense to rely on warm leads to grow your business, right? Actually, no. Warm leads from word of mouth and referrals are highly unpredictable, and they're not scalable. If your pipeline dries up, there's very little you can do. You can't turn on referrals like you can with paid ads, so it's hard to get them when you need them.

In the best-case scenario, you're stuck reaching out to clients and saying something like: "Our business depends on referrals from our great clients—do you know anyone that needs our services?" If you're lucky, you'll get an answer. More likely, you won't.

So it's paid leads all the way, then? Obviously not, because these can be very expensive to generate. SEO, for its part, can take a long, long time to produce results—and those results are far from guaranteed.

Let's not get depressed now. Here's what I've learned from targeting a dozen different niches over my twenty years as an entrepreneur: there's a *different* type of lead out there—the raving fan.

Exhibit 8

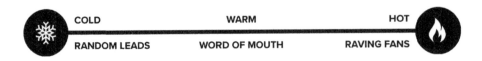

You already know how random leads and referrals show up. But when raving fans show up, they usually say something like this: "I've been following you for ages. I read everything you put out. I swear, it's like you're inside my head watching me work. I've put off moving forward for too long. I know it's going to be an investment, but I'm ready to get started."

Raving fans come in ready to buy, and they view your company as an authority—and as the only one that can help with their problems. I don't know about you, but I love those kinds of leads even better than referrals.

There's more to enjoy about these hot leads: while a referral is usually quicker to buy and more enjoyable to work with than a cold prospect, a raving fan is the *best of all* to work with.

Raving fans come in educated about what you do and how you do it. They've studied who you are, and in their minds, you're a celebrity—one made just for them and the problems they're having with their businesses.

In one extreme case, a raving fan of mine tossed a credit card at me before I had even really met him—joking, "Just take my money." It was, to say the least, a joyful experience—and an experience I want for you.

To be viewed as an authority, you need four things:

1. Proof of results

2. Third-party endorsements

3. Message recognition

4. Influencer association

I'll explain each of these below and then discuss how they build on each other to create even more leverage.

Proof of Results

You can get far in any market by being able to "talk the talk," as we discussed in the last chapter on attraction. Eventually, however, people are going to wonder if you also "walk the walk."

Do you have any proof of how awesome you are? As I told Heather, leads need you to do two things in the sales process: quantify the benefits of what they're thinking of buying and mitigate the risk of purchasing from you.

You need to prove, in other words, that your client will see a *real benefit* from their investment. Can they visualize a return? And can you help them become willing to take a risk? What assurance do they have that they aren't throwing their money in the trash?

Here's the good news. Unlike the stock market, where what happened yesterday or last year means nothing, a service firm's past performance is a *strong* predictor of future performance.

In other words, if you've done something before, people are likely to believe you can do it again. This kind of proof of performance can come in different flavors:

- Testimonials
- Case studies
- Portfolio examples
- Stories

- Professional history
- Stats
- Results
- Endorsements
- Accreditation
- Education

Communicating that you are an authority is a continuous process—one that refers to pieces of proof like the ones above in almost every conversation you have and piece of content you create. Proof should be a thread you weave through everything you do.

Always, always, always ask yourself two questions:

1. How am I proving that I can get my client measured benefits?

2. How am I proving that I'm not a risk for my client's investment?

And then answer those questions. Constantly.

Here's What Proof Looks Like

Let me show you how this works. Imagine for a moment you know nothing about me—I'm just a random guy you found on the internet. So I say, "Use my website proposal template on your next deal."

Immediately, you'll probably think, "Who is this guy? I'm not going to trust him with my financial future. What if I use this template and lose the deal I'm trying to land?" That line of thought would be completely logical. I haven't presented any specific benefit to using my template, so it seems really risky. The fear of losing thousands of dollars far outweighs the benefit of saving a little time by not having to create your own template.

But now let's add a bit of proof to help mitigate risk: "I pitched over 960 website deals in ten years. Use my website proposal template on your next deal." By adding a *proof point*, I've made my proposition seem a lot less risky.

Now you're probably thinking, "Well, he must have learned *something* from trying that many times. Maybe I'll check it out—he might be an expert that can teach me something."

But that first proof point only helps *mitigate the risk*, so let's look add another that *quantifies the benefit*: "I pitched over 960 website deals in ten years. Save hours of your time by using my website proposal template on your next deal—the same template I used to land a $22,864 project."

Now, *that's* compelling.

My proposition has gone from risky—possibly damaging—to credible and valuable. I'm providing the same resource as I was before, but now it has a much higher perceived value attached to it and a much lower level of risk.

This is the power of proof. That's why proof should appear everywhere—from the first sentence you communicate to your prospective clients to the last.

It should be a part of the headline on your website. Your value proposition. Your service descriptions. Your "About" page. Your case studies, success stories, and testimonials. Everywhere.

Proof points are also useful when:

- Producing content like blog posts, articles, or videos.
- Introducing yourself on a webinar, a podcast, or a stage.
- Telling people what you do.
- Delivering a talk from the stage.

- Updating your social profiles, and more.

Exhibit 9 is an example from the article I keep referring to:[16]

Exhibit 9

Never Say WordPress When Selling a Web Design Project

Building Your Proof Points

Whenever I ask my clients to tell me about their proof points, they get humble—shy, even. And even brave and engaged clients end up sounding like Eeyore, the clinically depressed donkey from the Winnie the Pooh books.

"Nobody cares about what I've done. After all, I'm not that great." Ugh!

Stop it right now. I don't care if you don't have experience in the market you want to serve. This is about the experience you *do* have—because past performance helps predict future success.

Now, as long as we're talking about Winnie the Pooh, I'm not suggesting you end up like Tigger—the tiger who has such a high view of himself that he sings a song about how wonderful he is.

But you need to be more like him than you may be comfortable with. There's no getting around it—you need to prove you're great. To do so, it can help to sit down and brainstorm some proof points.

My good friend and branding expert extraordinaire, Re Perez of Branding for the People, taught me to unpack proof points in five distinct buckets:

- *Functional.* What kind of experience do you have?

- *Social.* What good have you done? How have you helped others?

- *Economic.* What money or time can you make or save?

- *Credentials.* What certifications, awards, or degrees do you have?

- *Testimonials.* What case studies, big clients, or reviews do you have?

Try to start with at least three to seven proof points within each category. Yes, it's going to be hard. At first, you'll feel like you're bragging, but just get your proof on the page and sort it out later.

If you're still bashful, remember that you'll never include all of these points in a single paragraph. You're essentially building a menu that you can pull from later on in your content. Need examples? Here are some I've done over the years:

- *Functional*
  - I've been an entrepreneur for 19 years.
  - I created my first website when I was 15 years old.
- *Social*
  - My agency donated over $100,000 in pro bono services to charitable nonprofits.

○ We raised over $500,000 for Dr. Rick Hodes to help children in Ethiopia get life-saving spine surgery.

- *Economic*

  ○ We have generated over $10 million in revenue.

  ○ We managed more than 300 active clients at our agency.

- *Credentials*

  ○ We were named one of the top 10 fastest-growing companies (two years) by the *Denver Business Journal*.

  ○ I was a two-time Adobe MAX Speaker.

- *Testimonials*

  ○ Our clients ranged from start-ups to billion-dollar, publicly traded companies like Dish and Anheuser-Busch InBev.

  ○ We built the top training platform for Adobe's Business Catalyst system.

Looking for a worksheet you can use to collect proof points?

Download the Get Rich In The Deep End Field Guide: www.ownyourmarket.com/guide

What to Do with Your Proof Points

When you're done, a place to start is your website's "About" page. Try adding at least three of your proof points into the content you already have. Don't feel the need to rewrite the whole page—just sprinkle a few proof points into what you already have. (Use them like salt and pepper. Too much can make your "About" page unpalatable, but if you've done things right, your content will be "tastier.")

Try to include at least two number-based proof points. When people scan content, they're often drawn to numbers first, even if they don't end up reading anything else.

Now, compare the "before" and "after" versions of your "About" page. Which of them makes you seem more credible? Yes, of course—it's the one with the proof points added.

Special Kinds of Proof Points

You can quantify benefits and mitigate risk all day long, but it's a whole different story when a customer does it for you. Even still, most people freeze up when they think about asking a client for a testimonial or a case study.

That's why I like to ask these kinds of questions:

- "What were some problems you had before hiring us?"
- "How did our service help your business?"
- "Can you tell me about any tangible ROI you've received so far?"
- "Any other benefits?"
- "Were there any concerns you had before buying that turned out not being a big deal?"

These questions don't typically intimidate people—which means you can often turn their answers into a testimonial or a case study.

Use this format for either:

- Problem
- Solution
- Benefit

You want clients saying, "We had this problem, we were offered this solution, and we got this benefit." Remember to keep things short: testimonials only need to be about three to five sentences. You can get away with the same number of paragraphs for case studies. Please don't write twenty pages!

Try to get the benefits up-front. I see too many agencies put their client's name as the headline. Then, buried beneath the weight of a thousand words, is something like: "Our social media strategy helped generate a 2,775% ROI on our client's ad spend." That's the *hook!* Bring that juicy awesomeness to the top!

Here's the critical thing to remember, whether you're writing a case study or testimonial: every project has proof points, so use them! Your customer story will be much more compelling when it's packed with proof. (Hint: you could even use the same worksheet from the Field Guide to collect them.)

Again—testimonials and case studies aren't about bragging. They're about saying, "I know what I'm doing. I've driven past results that can predict how your project will turn out in the future. As you can see, I'm a safe investment for your business."

Get those proof points on.

Third-Party Endorsements

To most of your leads, you're a stranger. And because humans have been hardwired over millennia to depend on our social groups for safety, we resist trusting strangers. If you think you can walk into the market you are targeting and, *as a stranger,* convince people to do business with you, you've got a hard road ahead.

You know you're not a threat and that you just want to serve, but *your leads* don't. You need to rely on third-party endorsements— influential people saying good things about you.

Think of a guy in a bar. If he approaches a woman and says: "I'm handsome. We should go out on a date," he'll likely get a drink to the face.

But that conversation will probably go differently if the woman's friend tells her, "Hey, look at that handsome guy at the end of the bar. You should ask him out." Our barfly has gone from being creepy to being someone worthy of at least a little attention.

The bottom line? Third-party endorsements help strangers trust you. That's why making an active effort to get them is essential to your business. Here are the endorsements in Exhibit 10 that we use on our own website:

Exhibit 10

Look at that collection of logos.

How do they make you feel? If you're in the agency business, you've probably heard some of those names. You might even be a customer of some of those companies. And if you trust *them,* now you trust *us* just a little bit more.

How to Get Endorsements

The easiest way to get third-party endorsements is publishing on other influencers' platforms. While this isn't the most potent "thumbs-up" you can get, you can likely snag one with little experience within your market. Just like Heather.

When someone publishes your content, they're saying, "We believe in this person's message enough to broadcast it." They're acting here as a filter: their audience trusts them to bring the best ideas to their platform. That means they're more likely to assume a post of mine is high-quality, relevant material.

Interviews can also help this way. When you're featured with someone influential, you seem a little more influential yourself. If you get interviewed on a popular podcast in your niche, some of the interviewer's reputation rubs off on you. If their audience trusts them, they're also likely to trust you after the interview.

The best part is that getting published or interviewed can often lead to more robust endorsements:

- Keynote presentations
- Feature articles or reviews *about* you (not written *by* you)
- Social mentions
- Direct promotion by others (email, webinars, etc.)
- Celebrity or influencer mentions
- Certifications or accreditations

Endorsements are *so* powerful that I recommend you aim for six to twelve of them when you're first starting out in a market. This number provides enough credibility that prospects more easily check off the "authority" box in their minds when they first show up to your business.

"Brent, what about logos?" It's a question I often hear. Logos from publishers, associations, and influencers will likely be familiar to leads, which means associating yourself with these brands can instantly lift the reputation of your business.

And, gosh, if it needs to be repeated—this isn't about bragging. You're merely saying to prospective customers, "Look, I'm safe! I'm not some dangerous intruder! These other people say I'm a friend!" And that helps you get accepted by your audience quickly and without friction. Look at Exhibit 11 to see an example of how endorsements have the power to create instant credibility.

Exhibit 11

But you'll want to stay away from client logos. Unless your clients are well-known, most people visiting your website will have no idea who those companies are.

What to Do When You Start Getting Endorsements

As you get more and more prestigious endorsements, make sure you add them to your content, just like you would with proof points.

I was recently introducing a speaker and was able to tell my audience, "She is a writer for *Forbes*" because she is a member of their contributor program. Almost everyone knows who *Forbes* is—and that immediately established her as an authority.

But even if you're not writing for *Forbes* yet, don't resist this type of self-promotion because the benefits can come instantly. It took me all of about three months, from February 2013 to April 2013 to become known widely within the web professional and digital agency market.

For another example, look to Nate Freedman—the man behind Tech Pro Marketing, the company you see in the picture above. He went from being "nobody" in the IT and MSP market to being invited to publish on almost every platform in his niche within three months.

Crazy, huh? It can happen that fast.

Message Recognition

You may think you need to come up with new material and messaging constantly, so let me be clear: you don't. You simply need to get your main message *recognized.*

I was talking with an advisor of mine right after I had given a talk on selling higher-value projects. The presentation was a runaway success, and like most people who find success with one thing, I was convinced I could be successful with anything.

So I started talking about what I was going to do next—when he stopped me. He said, "Brent, you could spend the rest of your life telling people about selling higher-value projects, and you'd still never run out of people to teach."

That has always stuck with me, and it helps me resist the temptation to rush on to a new message. After all, there are *so many people* who haven't heard my *main* message!

 **Repeat your core message often. It'll take at least 7 times before your audience hears anything for the first time.**

When I first launched UGURUS' Bootcamp program, I *almost* fell into the "what's next" trap. We thought, "Okay, we did that. Now let's build another product and sell it just like that!"

We had thirty-four people sign up for our first program. That's out of somewhere between 250,000 and 1,000,000 potential customers around the world. (And at the time, only 10,000 of them were on our email list.)

Thankfully, I realized I didn't need to come up with a new message. I didn't need a new product or service. I needed to get the word out to many, many, many more people. I needed to keep doing what I was doing over and over again.

There is a saying that goes, "You have to hear something seven times before you hear it for the first time."[17] That, in turn, reminds me of a Latin proverb: *repetitio est mater studiorum*. In English, that means "Repetition is the mother of learning."[18]

"Repetition is the mother of learning."

"Repetition is the mother of learning."

"Repetition is the mother of learning."

"Repetition is the mother of learning."

"Repetition is the mother of learning."

"Repetition is the mother of learning."

See what I did there?

Here's the truth: most of your audience isn't paying attention to you. I mean, are you *really* paying attention to everyone you follow? Do you read *every* email that comes into your inbox with a highlighter, ready to take notes and catalog the information?

Of course not. You scan. You review. You tune out. You go to the restroom. You get distracted.

Here's an example. I've seen my friend Joey Coleman's talk on "The First 100 Days" a dozen times.[19] Every time I watch it, I pick up just a little more of what he's trying to teach me. It probably took me five times before I started to see the light.

That's the beauty of repetition. Your newer customers will feel like they're hearing your message for the first time, and your best customers will value the reinforcement.

The only people in your audience who will be annoyed are the information hoarders. They're not interested in *learning* and *applying* what you are saying—only accumulating the most information in their brains and notebooks.

Don't worry about these people. If you want to appease them, you can make small tweaks to your material—tell some new stories, show new examples—but don't change your core message, or you'll risk losing message recognition.

Remember—you may need to repeat your message seven times or more to each person before it's finally heard. Stop trying to be so creative! Once you identify the top three problems you solve and have a useful solution for each, stop adding to your service offering.

Instead, get out there and repeat that message over and over until you tire of it. Then do it some more. Rather than inventing new problems or new services, look for more places to talk about the same old stuff.

Yes, you can slowly *evolve* within your platform, but once you find something that works within your market, stay the course.

Influencer Association

When you have authority in your market, you'll start getting opportunities that are reserved for "market influencers." And by getting these opportunities, you can rest assured that other people in your market will view you as an authority.

Now, you can't control whether other influencers and platforms start reaching out to offer coveted spots on their blogs, podcasts, social channels, and stages. But you *can* significantly increase the odds of this happening by building a list of influencers in your market and establishing relationships with them.

Humans are tribal creatures, as I've explained, and they have a "herd mentality" when it comes to trusting one another.

This means that if you build relationships with influencers and find ways to publicly collaborate—perhaps a podcast interview, livestream, or blog content—your market will begin to perceive you as an influencer.

Now, before you freak out about approaching influencers and "micro-celebrities," remember that they're people, just like you. At some point, they started out with zero followers, zero people on their email list, and zero customers. But they committed to a market and a set of problems and got to work building their audience and reputation—and that's what got them where they are today.

Look past the shining lights, though. Ignore the accolades, and the likes and retweets, and the published books. Influencers have personal issues, business issues, and everything in between—like we all do.

And this might surprise the heck out of you, but a lot of influencers have a hard time making money. Just because someone *looks* like they have it all figured out doesn't mean they know what they're doing.

Here are common problems that influencers face:

- Struggle to monetize their list, fan-base, and website traffic
- Have a limited amount of time and resources to do what they want
- Can't keep up with the constant demand for content

I once worked with an influencer who was seeing over one million website visitors a month, but he couldn't monetize those viewers—he didn't have what he needed to turn them into buyers.

For some reason, he believed that his audience didn't have any money to spend. So every time he launched a product, he sold them for low-dollar amounts like $12 or $27. His thought was that since he had so much traffic, he needed to create products and services for as much of his audience as possible.

But his efforts weren't enough. He was bleeding cash and unable to fund his operations. On the outside, none of this was visible. His email list, traffic stats, and social feeds were all super active and impressive.

At the time, my core offer was about $3,000—and I knew it would appeal to only a sliver of his audience. But a sliver of one million is still a big number, so I wanted to try.

I proposed that if he promoted a webinar for our program to his list, I would give him a percentage of revenue. We ended up onboarding twenty-three clients from the campaign—and he doubled his monthly revenue *for two months* on the strength of the commissions.

That was a benefit for both of us.

The exciting part? You can set up the same kind of situation for yourself. Here are five steps to help you leverage existing influencers in your market:

1. *First, build a list.* Building a list of influencers is similar to building a list of publishers or associations within your market.

   But influencers are people, not just websites. Occasionally, they work for an existing company or organization—and might not be the company itself.

   They usually have access to some kind of publishing platform, but not always.

   And they could simply be super-connectors with large networks.

   Go past the platform or website and start looking for the individuals who are doing the writing, hosting, and streaming. Find their social profiles. (Even if influencers aren't the owners of the websites or platforms they're publishing on, they likely own their own social media accounts.)

   From there, you can find ways to get in touch with them.

2. *Follow your influencers and engage with them. It's* best if influencers are somewhat comfortable with you before you start reaching out and trying to find ways to work with them.

After you identify a list of influencers, follow them on social media. Engage with the content they are sharing. Reshare it yourself and see how you can add value to their platform without asking for something in return. For most influencers, engaging and sharing their material is the best compliment you can give them.

Once you've spent some time following and engaging, even if you haven't outright "met" the influencer on your list, they'll begin to know who you are. Most influencers pay close attention to those that engage with them and share their content.

(Bonus: This approach also gives you time to learn about them and their platform within your market.)

3. *Make contact and explore collaboration opportunities.* After a certain amount of engagement, you should have a good grasp on who your influencer is and what's important to them. This will be helpful when it's time to reach out.

There is no magic formula for how long you should follow and engage before you make first outward contact. In some cases, it could be a matter of days or weeks. In others, it could be months. Typically, you'll want to wait until you've been recognized a few times in the comments that they've made on their social channels.

Reaching out is pretty simple. You both serve the same market, which gives you an obvious reason to connect with them. Simply reaching out with something like this usually does the trick: "Hey, I've been following you for some time and see we both serve the same market. I'd love to figure out ways we can collaborate. Would you be open to a call so I could get to know more about what you're up to?"

You can modify this message to find what works for your voice and style and for the specific influencer you're reaching out to. It never hurts to add a sprinkle of context to the message and bring up some piece of content or social interaction that you had with them.

4. *Build a relationship.* It probably goes without saying, but you have to spend time building relationships with influencers. Learn about what they're up to, what their business is, and how they make money. Do your best to add value if you can.

   This could mean helping them connect with others you've met in the market, figuring out ways you can promote their material, or something else.

   Here's a caution, though: it's important when building a relationship with an influencer—with anyone, really— that you're careful about having an agenda. If people get the idea that you are just trying to sell them or get access to their audience, they might put up barriers or walls. This means that you might have to be patient when it comes to helping propel your own business.

   Even then, you also need to be okay with the possibility of that never happening. Some of the best relationships I have with influencers in my market have never transformed into a tangible promotion or public-facing event.

   And that's all right, too—you can exchange all sorts of other value.

5. *Explore collaboration opportunities.* Most influencers peddle some kind of content as a way to build their authority in their market, just like you do. That makes co-creating

content one of the simplest ways to build mutual trust with an influencer.

If you have a blog or podcast, this is an easy win. You can offer up your platform as a way to help them—and also get the benefit of the association. If they have a platform, you can offer ways to contribute value without necessarily receiving recognition.

Since influencers are usually looking to share their content with more and more people, you can often get them to agree to be interviewed or featured on your site, as that will help their platform. It also shows them that you aren't just looking to get access to their audience, you are willing to put them in front of yours, too. (No matter how small your audience is, this gesture speaks volumes.)

The more trust you build with your influencer network, the more possibilities will be available to you. I often go back to guests who have been on my podcast and invite them to do joint ventures where they promote our products and services to their lists. These types of relationships require a high level of trust, of course, but they can pay off big in the future.

Why go through all this work? Because once you've come to be associated with a few influencers in your market, you'll start to be perceived by your market as one yourself.

It doesn't matter how small your audience is, or how little time you've spent in your market. When you're seen with the established influencers in your market, their status will transfer to you.

You'd be surprised how little is required to start receiving the benefits of influencer association—especially if your content and ideas resonate with the influencer. Most influencers are well-connected and know other influencers. Get in with the right ones and you'll quickly find yourself asked to connect with other influencers.

That's the goal.

Instead of spending years developing your own platform, you can stand on the shoulders of the giants already established in your market and leverage their status to speed up the process of becoming an authority.

Chapter Eleven Take Aways to Get Rich In The Deep End

◆ Becoming an authority in your market has all sorts of benefits. More leads. Faster sales. Higher prices. It's worth the investment.

◆ Referrals are great. What most agencies are missing are *raving fans.*

◆ You haven't lived until you've signed a raving fan as a client.

◆ What you've done for other clients is a strong predictor of your performance with future clients. If you've solved these problems for other people exactly like your next lead, that's a powerful sales tool.

◆ When you talk about results your clients got, use a PSB framework: *problem, solution, and benefit.* Identify the problem the client had, unpack your solution, and follow through with the benefit your client achieved.

◆ Telling people, you're awesome is great. Having respected authorities in your market say the same things about you is next level awesome.

◆ Publishing on 3rd party's websites and platforms is an indirect way to get an endorsement. They are giving you a "thumbs up" when they publish you.

◆ Treat every endorsement just like you do with each piece of content. Celebrate it. Share it. Brag about it. Remind your market and list know how awesome you are.

◆ Repeat your core message often. It'll take at least 7 times before your audience hears anything for the first time.

◆ If you have the right message, wait for your market to tell you they've heard it enough (pro tip: they never will).

◆ Producing content with established influencers makes you an influencer by association.

CHAPTER TWELVE

Heather Acquires New Leads

As the barista pulled my double espresso, I glanced at my watch. Heather was late for the first time since I started working with her. Was she going to stand me up?

I knew the assignment I'd given her was outside her comfort zone. I've only ever had a few clients who weren't resistant to doing customer development. Years ago, I had been too. Back when I was selling websites for a living, I never spoke with prospective clients in a non-sales context. I was always pitching.

Everything changed when I learned how to interview prospective customers as a research and validation tool—not just for the purposes of selling. Almost overnight, I discovered the real pains and problems my market was experiencing. People let me in on what they were really thinking.

I got inside their heads.

This is what I had wanted for Heather. It was the missing link between knowing about business coaches and truly understanding them. But I did worry she thought it was some kind of punishment.

There had been a method to my madness, of course. When you talk to one or two people in your market, their individual biases steal the show. Once you speak to ten or more, patterns emerge. However, you can't see those patterns unless you do the interviews as fast as you can; your brain has a harder time making unconscious connections when you space your meetings too far out.

In other words, the more customer development you do in a short amount of time, the more you increase your odds of entrepreneurial magic. Heather needed some of that magic. But two weeks had passed since our last meeting—and I had no idea how she had done.

As I gently brought my drink to a table, movement outside the window caught my eye. There was Heather—walking briskly to the café's entrance. She burst into the café in a flurry of excitement.

 ### Whisper the right things in the right places.

"Brent! I'm so sorry I'm late. You won't believe this, but I just finished my tenth customer development interview. I'm late because she just kept going on and on and on. I have seven pages of notes! She would hardly let me ask her my interview questions. She just wanted to hire me! And I had to keep saying *no*!"

I won't lie—I was more than a little relieved.

"That's great news, Heather. I'm so proud that you took action. I had put the odds that you wouldn't show today at about 50–50. It's happened before."

Heather shook her head with a smile on her face. "Brent, you've opened up a whole new world for me. I can't believe I've gone this long and never sat down with prospective customers when there wasn't a pitch at the end of the process. Just focusing on learning from them changes everything."

As Heather told me more and more, I started to feel what drew me to this type of consulting and coaching in the first place. I love seeing people get tangible results in their business. But nothing—and I mean nothing—in my line of work comes close to the joy of watching someone change their deeply held erroneous beliefs.

I knew I would never learn everything that Heather discovered in her time doing customer development. But I also knew she wouldn't, either. At least not right away. Deep within her mind, she had already cataloged anecdotes, hints about tone and body language, and insights that would only become apparent to her as she dove deeper and deeper into her marketing activities.

Then Heather paused as if she was about to tell me something big. "Brent, the other night, after I got home from one of my interviews, I wrote a brand-new article. Two thousand words! I talked about a problem I had heard time and again during my interviews—something that's keeping my audience up at night.

"I cut to the bone of that problem. It's the big fear that I know how to solve—and I spelled out exactly how in this article. Plus, I spoke my customers' language, and I brought in my proof points, too. And then I submitted it to the publisher that keeps rejecting me.

"And they emailed this morning: they're going to publish the article in a couple of weeks as a feature! It's going to be in their weekly email that goes out to over a hundred thousand coaches across the globe!"

For the first time in a long while, I was speechless. For Heather, the game of business was about to change. Then a worried look came over her face. "Brent—what's next? Seriously, I hope you have something up your sleeve to help me capture leads better. I'm not prepared for this type of exposure."

I looked down at my empty espresso cup. "Sure, let's talk about the fifth A: Acquire.

"But you seem like you're on a whole other level this morning." I smiled. "I'll need another espresso first."

Redesign

Heather's website was like just about every other agency site on the planet: a kitchen soup homepage that could appeal to any type of business, a services page that listed every skill and deliverable imaginable that her team could perform, an "About" page that was all about them and not her clients, and a generic contact us form and phone number.

I had known since the start that Heather needed a different type of website. But I had also always been aware that she had ten years of momentum behind the EMA site—and the last thing I wanted her to do was to turn that off.

Trouble was, she also had less than two weeks to get her redesign right. Fortunately, she felt some of this tension, too. "Brent, I think I should totally revamp my entire website. Is it time to change my homepage to focus exclusively on business coaches?"

No, I said, there was no need to draw a line in the sand just yet.

On the one hand, shutting down the current site made sense. But Heather also had a large payroll to support, and she wasn't yet getting the traction she needed in the business coach market to go all-in (yet).

What she needed was a lightweight marketing asset that served a narrow purpose for her market. She also needed to shift her thinking about where her website fit in her client-acquisition system.

So I asked her a question instead—what percentage of her client base comprised business coaches? Heather thought for a moment. "It's small, I guess. I've just had a few articles published. We've been around for a decade as an agency, but as you know, the shift to coaches is new."

"Okay," I said. "Let's keep your existing EMA website as-is for now. If you think of marketing as one of those plate-spinning acts you see on the TV variety shows, then your current EMA site is like one plate. You may wish you didn't have to focus attention on it, but right now we need to keep it spinning. After all, it does accomplish something.

"So instead of thinking about replacing what you have, let's think in terms of adding to it."

Heather looked down at her laptop screen on the café table. "I could add a landing page focused entirely on business coaches. Is that what you mean?"

I smiled. "Yes. We can create a dedicated micro-site within your current brand that you can start to link to from external articles and advertising traffic. Its sole purpose will be to generate qualified coaching leads for your business."

"When more of your business comes from the business coach market than your core agency business now, then you can look at transitioning to that market or even creating a separate market-focused brand."

"But for now, let me walk you through how to create an appointment funnel and lead magnet."

Getting Leads

When we met again two weeks later, I have to admit—I had been really hoping Heather had done her homework.

After all, her big article had gone live—"3 Secrets Helping the Top Business Coaches Dominate Online"—and I would have been devastated if she had missed the chance to get some leads.

But sure enough, when she showed me the article, there it was: her byline and a link back to her specific "/coaches" landing page on her EMA website. I clicked on the link to find a compelling, focused headline aimed directly at coaches: "You're a top business coach. Too bad your marketing is holding you back."

A few lines below that unpacked the problems Heather had discovered during her customer interviews. Case study snippets touted her work, and she had included social proof from Amy's project—plus a nice before-and-after screenshot.

 **Tapping into other people's audiences is the fastest way to put your message in front of hundreds, thousands, or even millions of people overnight.**

I scanned further and found—yes!—a big fat "schedule an appointment" button. Heather had positioned it as a "breakthrough session" to help coaches determine whether their website and marketing were holding their business back.

Further down the page, there was an opportunity to sign up to receive a bonus download—a free high-value document. I sat back in the café chair with a giant grin. "You got it all done, Heather. Excellent job following the recipe.

"And I saw the social share numbers on the side of the publisher's page. You've got a big hit on your hands! How does it feel?"

With a conspiratorial look on her face, Heather pulled out her own laptop and placed it on the table as she pulled a chair around to my side. "Brent, I need you to see this," she said in a stage whisper. "It's crazy. I've never experienced anything like it."

She opened her calendar app and showed me a solid block of six qualification calls. The next week? Another six. And the week after that. And four the week after that.

"Brent, I have twenty-two appointments booked on my calendar from a single article. I have never in my life had even three sales calls schedule themselves on my calendar while I was off doing other things.

"I've already spoken to a few of these leads. Two of them need new websites and marketing plans—like yesterday. I signed one up for our strategy intensive. They gave me a credit card over the phone on our second call. And with the other, I'm waiting on a confirmation to move forward."

I was beside myself. "That's spectacular news. Let me shake your hand."

Heather spread her arms wide. "Forget about handshakes! This calls for a hug!"

After a couple of congratulatory pats on the back, I replied, "Well done, Heather. You did the work and now you're enjoying the results. But it ain't over. Don't take this the wrong way, but I need you to start on your next article immediately. Building a predictable pipeline of opportunity requires you to keep going."

Heather took her seat, still wide-eyed.

"Brent, that's the thing. They loved the article so much they've asked me to commit to a monthly piece! But that's not even it. There's one more thing. They want me to do a workshop at their upcoming conference, too! I'm in full-on 'freak out' mode, of course. I've never given a keynote presentation in my life. I have no idea what I'm doing."

I drained my espresso and smiled. "Well, Heather, our work is cut out for us. But you've got this."

Chapter Twelve Take Aways to Get Rich In The Deep End

- You learn about your market by talking to people.

- Discover patterns by immersing yourself in your target market. Have 10, 20, or even 100 conversations and you'll soon find you have an unofficial MBA for your niche.

- Niching is more than just updating your website's homepage. You need to get out in your market. Be recognized for something. Changing what your website says is almost the last thing that we do, not the first.

- I'd rather see one well-crafted sentence that speaks to our ideal client and a contact form–than a twenty-page agency website that speaks to no one with generic content.

- When it comes to marketing assets–like your website–start small, think landing page, not portfolio

CHAPTER THIRTEEN

The Fifth A—Acquire

The first four of the 5 A's are about helping you drive more people to your front door so you can *acquire* them as leads and customers. That's the fifth A—and, really, it's the whole reason you're doing any of this.

Because although getting attention in your market can feel exciting, you don't want to forget why you want attention in the first place:

So you can overcome the unpredictability of word of mouth and referrals and instead build a steady stream of leads who buy from you.

Now, when most people think about how to do that, they consider individual tactics like these:

- Calls to action.
- Direct offers for paid services.
- Links to other valuable content.
- Valuable opt-ins.
- Links to your website or landing page.
- Invitations to reach out, follow, or schedule a call.

And yes, depending on the channel and timing, each one of these could help you get the results you're looking for. However, the truth is none of them will work in isolation. If you expect people to magically discover you and then decide to offer you money on their own, you're dreaming.

Instead, you need to guide them to the sale with a well-oiled machine. You need a marketing engine.

Why a Marketing "Engine"?

Most people take the same view of marketing activities—as disconnected tactics with no central strategy. They also dilute their efforts by fueling too many ideas. Post to social media one day, give a keynote another, and guest-post another day.

I prefer to build a single system, drive traffic through it, optimize it, and see what kind of results I can get. I call that process building a "marketing engine." It's a good metaphor for what you need to do to acquire leads and customers.

A car's engine, obviously, won't work without both a source of fuel and someone to put that fuel in it. But when you add that fuel, you can step on the gas and create forward motion in the car.

Your marketing engine works the same way. The source of your fuel? An investment of your time and/or money to create a flow of people's attention commonly referred to as *traffic*. This attention must land on ads, landing pages, blog posts, or some piece of content designed to convert attention into action.

 **Every marketing engine has 5 stages: strategy, proven, repeatable, predictable, and scalable.**

By creating marketing conversions—those magical moments when a visitor changes into a lead or a scheduled appointment— you're "stepping on the gas," revving up the RPMs, and moving your business forward with conversations. The more conversations you have with ideal prospects from your market, the more likely you are to gain speed with sales and revenue.

If any of the critical parts are missing, the engine won't get you where you want to go. Without any fuel, you're not going anywhere, whether you have all the parts or not. If you don't step on the gas, your engine won't do *anything*—and your speed will be zero.

How to Make Your Marketing Engine Work

You need an engine, and you need to make sure it works like this (Exhibit 12):

Exhibit 12

MARKETING ENGINE PLANNER™: **Brent Weaver @ UGURUS**

NICHE: **Digital agencies**   CHANNEL: **Guest Blogging**

Traffic Source	Awareness Event	Conversion Driver	Conversation Mechanism
AMI (publisher)	Guest Blog Posts	**PRIMARY** Strat Call Application & Scheduler	Intro / Strategy Call
DesignModo (publisher)		**SECONDARY** Lead Magnet Email Opt-In	Email List
Paid FB ads			
Email List			

EXAMPLE

Key Measurables:
* Reach/traffic
* Email list size
* Posts committed

Fuel Activities:
* Publisher research
* Publisher pitches

Key Measurables:
* Posts published

Fuel Activities:
* Writing guest posts

Key Measurables:
* Strat call applications
* Strat call scheduled
* Email addresses opted in

Key Measurables:
* Calls held
* Discoveries won
* Emails on list

Results:
* Have strat / intro call

UGURUS

For an editable version of this template, download the Get Rich In The Deep End Field Guide at OwnYourMarket.com/Guide.

As you can see in the engine map above (Exhibit 12), there is a clear "line of sight" from traffic to sales—and a defined process that moves visitors step by step from hearing about you to buying from you.

To get your marketing engine working for you so you can "drive" your sales, you'll have to do six things:

1. Find a gas station. (Identify what kind of traffic you want.)

2. Fill up the tank. (Use awareness events to bring people to your site.)

3. Turn on the car. (Convert visitors into interested leads.)

4. Put the car in Drive and step on the gas pedal. (Set appointments and make sales.)

5. Check to make sure you're going in the right direction. (Measure your results.)

6. Tinker with the engine to keep it running optimally. (Improve what's working and fix what isn't.)

Don't worry if that doesn't make sense yet—I'll explain each of those six things now.

1. Find a Gas Station (aka, Identify Your Traffic Source)

First, identify your fuel sources. If you plan to get on podcasts, build a list of every podcast that touches your market. If you want to guest-post, build a list of publishers. Love to speak on stages? Build a list of every stage relevant to your market.

Now, not every audience and awareness channel are equal. Some have more people you can reach than others. And there certainly isn't only one source of traffic in the market you serve—I guarantee it.

You're going to be tempted to look at multiple channels, but trust me. The smarter way is to focus on only one to start. I'll explain later in this chapter. For now, build a traffic source plan—and then stick to the plan, even when the going gets good.

2. Fill Up the Tank (aka, Start with Your Awareness Events)

Great! You've found a channel! But you're still only at the "gas station." You have to put that gas *into the engine* for it to do its stuff. In other words, you might have compiled a list of ways to get your message out—but that doesn't mean you'll end up with leads.

First, you have to get someone to let you share your message in those places. Then you have to use those opportunities to make your audience aware of the problems they have and credibly position yourself as a solution.

That's why this part of the process will require an investment of your time or money—I shouldn't have to explain that most marketing is about carrying out awareness activities like publishing guest posts, doing podcasts, or speaking on stages—over and over again.

Building a list of blogs or podcasts is just the first step. Getting access to those audiences requires you to invest the time to build relationships with the publishers or hosts, create valuable content, and stay consistent in repeating this outreach activity over and over. The same is true if you are advertising. If you have an ad that works, you have to put the money in the meter week after week to keep getting the results.

When we first entered the digital agency market, we built our email list to more than ten thousand people. That didn't happen because we wrote *one* article. It was because we got published more than a *dozen* times in our niche within a few months.

To grow our email list to the size it is today, we've created more than a hundred publishing opportunities and spent hundreds of thousands of dollars on advertising.

That's a lot of fuel in the tank. And a lot of trips to the gas station, pumping over and over again. Don't get me wrong though—the process was never random or indiscriminate. Through it all, we focused on two factors.

Quantity of fuel. How much "gas" can you pump into your marketing engine? In other words, how many awareness activities can you pull off? The answer will depend on the size of your traffic source (list size, monthly visitors, people in the audience) and the frequency with which you can get in front of them (weekly, monthly, quarterly, or yearly).

When researching traffic sources, look for signs of size. Check their advertisers page or simply ask them. Often, organizations tout the size of their membership right on the home page, for example.

Increasing the extent to which you rely on a traffic source is one of the easiest ways to score additional awareness for your business.

Think about your own situation. Do you have a favorite website that you read often? Do you read *every* article that appears on the site? I don't. In the best case, I might read less than 5% of the content that a publisher in my niche puts out. And whether I read it has more to do with the headline and hook than the author.

It's not only *possible* to circle back to the same traffic source dozens of times in a year, but I strongly recommend it.

I've seen many experts speaking at the same conference every year; for example, I spoke at Adobe MAX and other Adobe events a half dozen times. Each talk, I brought a little different content on the same overall subject and earned more and more customers. The best part is that if you do a good job, it gets easier to be accepted.

Quality of fuel. The audience you're doing awareness activities for—how much does it resemble your chosen customer segment?

And what kind of relationship does the publisher or platform have with that audience? I've been published on platforms that were a tenth of the size of others—and seen ten times the results.

How? Message and market fit. Given a choice between a highly targeted audience that I know needs my service and a massive audience that's not really interested in what I have to offer, I'll choose the smaller audience every time.

In other words, context matters, but so does the relationship. I've had major publishers with massive lists promote our brand like crazy—with far less satisfactory results than other partners that had built close relationships with their lists.

It's hard to measure "relationships," of course, but to start, you ask partners about their email open rates or about how much money customers spend with your partner's brand.

Choosing where to fill your tank. Exhibit 13 is a worksheet you can use to plan how to fill your tank. For an editable copy, download the Get Rich In The Deep End Field Guide at OwnYourMarket.com/Guide.

Exhibit 13

Traffic Source		
Quantity	**Example**	**Your Opportunity**
Audience size	50.000	
Available frequency	Monthly	
Quality		
Customer segment	Ideal	
Relationship	Strong	
Content		
Five stages of funel	Yes	
Hook. Build. Payoff.	Yes	

3. Turn on the Engine (aka, Create Conversions)

Fuel is only *potential* energy. When it's in the gas pump—or even in your tank—it does nothing until you turn the engine on and put the pedal to the metal.

I can't tell you how many times I see entrepreneurs build lists of potential sources and then take no action. One friend of mine was struggling to get leads, so they mapped out a list of ten amazing conferences within their niche—only to register for zero.

They had a powerful race car at their disposal. They were on the racetrack. They had their foot on the pedal. They had everything they needed—but the business foundered anyway. Once awareness events start happening, you'll want to make sure you're getting conversions!

To create conversions, create a conversion driver. A conversion driver is a compelling offer for your audience to take the next step with you. The best ones directly generate a highly qualified sales conversation with an educated buyer.

But there are many more for different mediums and stages of the buying process. Here are some examples. (And, yes—these look a lot like the tactics I discussed at the beginning of this chapter. When they're used as part of a fully functioning marketing engine, they work wonders.)

- Call-to-action at the end of an article
- Link to a high-value download or "content upgrade"
- Free "strategy call" consultation
- Free course (video or email) that solves a real pain your customer is aware of
- Lower-cost offer with a substantial, "hard to refuse" discount

Here's what happens when you don't do that: I once gave a talk to three hundred people and didn't have a way to drive conversions. I said something like: "Thanks for having me. Come talk to me later if you want more information."

I had fuel in the tank. My foot was on the gas, but the engine just puttered out. Consequently, I got only a couple of leads—which didn't drive enough action to get a new paying customer. Sadly, the conference also happened to be in Australia—so I had plenty of time on the flight back to reflect on my poor performance.

Whatever your conversion driver is, it must push your audience to a conversion they *want*—not just one that you think they need. As the saying goes, "Give them what they want. Sell them what they need."

I once watched a great talk by a digital agency owner. She provided an insane amount of value—and her presentation was thought-provoking. But then, at the end of it, she made an offer for their company's paid services.

It wasn't a "sell from stage" moment, but it was close. She said something like: "If you need a new website, digital marketing services, strategy planning, or any of these services"—and she listed two dozen—"then give us a call."

She didn't realize she wasn't educating her audience—she was asking them to make a purchasing decision about a vast array of potential solutions.

It wasn't a "pitch" in her eyes—after all, she wasn't asking for money—but the thought process for her audience was the same. They were thinking: "Am I ready to invest in my website? My digital marketing? Not yet, I'll reach out later."

Did they? Of course not. They forgot about her whole offer by the end of the first break. Your conversion driver's job is *not* to sell your audience your core offer—it's to start the process that will eventually lead to you having a sales conversation. In other words, don't get fancy—all you need to do is ask for an appointment. (More on that below.)

What does a conversion driver look like? Here are some examples of conversion drivers in the wild.

Note that not all of them lead *directly* to a scheduled call. Those are the best ones, but you can also have a conversation over email, messenger apps, and social media channels—whatever works to get you in front of people and talking so that you can *eventually* ask for a sales conversation.

Article—Strategy Call

Exhibit 14

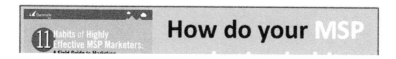

This, in essence, is how MSPs often waste money on the wrong type of marketing. You don't just need ANY digital marketing tactic to be successful. You need the right approach for the right audience at exactly the right time. The only way you're going to do that is by laying the solid foundation of a clear strategy first and then slowly but surely building on it from there.

Link to strategy call landing page

Do you often feel like you're "lost at sea" when it comes to marketing for your IT business? You're certainly not alone, but thankfully, you're also looking at a problem with a straightforward solution. If you feel like this describes your situation, I encourage you to apply for a one-on-one strategy call with us at Tech Pro Marketing. We'll dive deep into your business, helping you to uncover your own unique voice and purpose so we can provide real change in both your business and your life.

Article—Opt-in

Exhibit 15

Often I hear, "my clients really want mobile, but they aren't willing to pay for me to make the site responsive."

So what's the problem? Are we charging too much?

Link to high value content opt-in

What I Do Differently

When sitting with a client, my website proposal process involves a lot of discovery. I like to have three to four meetings with my clients to understand their business as well as I can. Much of the time I spend with them is finding the core pains that exist in their business and then building value for a solution that solves those pains.

This conversation often sounds like this:

"Why do you need a new website?"

"Our website is really outdated. It was designed by a friend of a friend several years ago and has fallen out of date."

Landing Page—Opt-in

Exhibit 16

Keynote—Free Course Plus Strategy Call

Exhibit 17

Thank You!

brent@ugurus.com
facebook.com/brentweaver

Incidentally, to help you see a conversion driver in the wild, I've created a landing page and four-part email series you can copy and use however you want in your business. You can sign up here: https://ownyourmarket.com/no-website-afterall-email-course.

Once you have your new conversion driver, follow up. No matter what kind of conversion driver I'm using, I aim to cast a wide net to get basic contact information so I can keep in touch with them, working on turning them into a customer.

Don't make the mistake of getting email addresses and failing to follow up with people. I often see people get twenty, one hundred, or even five hundred email addresses from a campaign, send them an initial series—and then forget the list exists.

In my business, I know that once I have an email, I have a good chance of eventually setting up a sales call with them. But that only happens because I follow up.

4. Put the Car in Drive and Step on the Gas Pedal
(aka, Set Appointments and Make Sales)

As you start to find traction with your fuel sources, awareness events, and conversion drivers, you'll need one more piece—a way to generate appointments. I call this a "conversation mechanism." Yes, conversation—be careful not to misread that as "conversion." A marketing engine creates *conversions* that drive *conversations.*

If you can't talk to a prospect one-on-one, then your secondary goal should be to get contact details. That way, you can nurture and educate them—in the hopes of getting another chance to schedule a conversation.

But conversations need to be your absolute priority.

Automate your conversation scheduling. Now, as you scale your activities, you won't want to do the back and forth with people to book an intro call. Having a conversation to figure out when to have a conversation is—well, it's a crazy waste of your time.

Get an automatic scheduling system in place, and that will free you up for the actual sales conversations. You could try a simple scheduler, like this one from Calendly in Exhibit 18:

Exhibit 18

But there are lots of scheduling tools out there. If you use a customer relationship management system (CRM), the choice might be more limited, but you can likely use a tool like Zapier to make a scheduler work with whatever you have.

Some people like to put an application form in front of their schedulers, as you see here (Exhibit 19):

Exhibit 19

Apply for a One on One Strategy Call

Do you ever feel like your marketing strategy has slowly gone off course? Do you feel like you're lost at sea without a map, let alone a paddle to help get you and your business where you need to go? What needs to change? What's holding you back?

Apply for a One on One call and find out: can Tech Pro Marketing help you?

Pre-call application form:

- ⊙ Please complete this quick and easy intake form so we can best determine if we are a good fit for each other
- ⊙ You'll receive an email within two business days of submitting this form about your appointment
- ⊙ Strategy calls should be done from a quiet location with limited distractions - please be prepared for a 60 minute strategy call

First Name *

Last Name *

Email *

Phone *

Website *

How did you find out about us? *

How much is an average client worth to you in a year? **

$0 - $2,500

Have you tried digital marketing in the past? *

Yes

No

Is there anything else you'd like us to know (optional)

MAKE AN APPOINTMENT

I recommend this approach if your time starts to become a premium—that is, if you're getting more leads than you have time for.

Schedule strategy calls, not sales meetings. You might have noticed the phrase "strategy call" above. I've used it throughout the book, but if you're not familiar with the term, let me explain.

A strategy call *isn't* your average "get to know you" introduction chat. Instead, it's a particular type of meeting that serves a specific purpose within your sales funnel.

And here's why you want to use them. For a typical business, the sales process starts when a potential customer fills out a lead form or picks up the phone. But for the business with a marketing engine in place, awareness events have usually moved that prospect all the way from unaware to solution-aware.

That means that the first conversation between business and lead can go deeper than it usually might. A *lot* deeper. Hence, a strategy call instead of your standard "qualification" call. How to actually *conduct* a strategy call is beyond the scope of this book, but here's a brief outline of how I do mine:

1. Set the stage (get commitment).
2. Qualify (if necessary).
3. Help them see they're on the "Island of Sad"—a place in their business they don't want to stay anymore.
4. Show them what it would be like to live on the "Island of Happy"—the place they're trying to get to.
5. Ask their permission, then show them how I can be the bridge that helps them get from one place to the other.
6. Reflect their needs and wants as a summary.
7. Ask their permission, then lay out their investment of time & money.

8. *Stop talking* and let them take over to tell you where their objections are.

9. Overcome objections.

10. Win the engagement *or*

11. Schedule the next appointment.

Even just from looking at this outline, you can probably guess that your main job with a strategy call is to identify the pains and problems your customer is experiencing and their desired outcomes.

You want to find out their goals, objectives, and dreams. Then you'll determine if you can solve their problem, and if so, you want to make an initial pitch.

From there, you can overcome objections or schedule additional time for other decision-makers or stakeholders to get involved.

If you're interested in learning more about strategy calls, download the Get Rich In The Deep End Field Guide at OwnYourMarket.com/Guide.

5. Check to Make Sure You're Going in the Right Direction (aka, Measure Results)

Once you've built your marketing engine and it's starting to run, don't forget to monitor the results it's producing.

To keep things simple, you should track no more than three to five simple measures—one or two is fine for each part of your engine.

Here are some examples:

- *Traffic sources:* ad dollars spent, guest posts written or published, guest podcasts booked, conference keynotes booked, and so on

- *Awareness events:* webinar attendees, lead magnet pageviews, attendees in the audience, etc.

- *Conversions:* opt-ins to your email list, contact form inquiries, etc.

- *Appointments and sales:* strategy calls booked, revenue generated, number of clients earned, and so on

Here's what those might look like for a guest-posting strategy (Exhibit 20):

Exhibit 20

INITIAL METRICS	MATURE METRICS (Once things are reliably up and running)
# of guest posts written # of guest posts published # of page views driven # of strategy calls booked # of clients earned	# of guest posts published (fuel) # of strategy calls booked (rpm) # of clients earned (speed)

If you were advertising a webinar on Facebook, those measures might look something like this (Exhibit 21):

Exhibit 21

INITIAL METRICS	MATURE METRICS
# of ad dollars spent # of webinar attendees # of applications # of strategy calls booked # of clients earned	# of ad dollars spent # of applications # of clients earned

Metrics matter because they empower you to stop focusing on "everything"—and concentrate only on adding fuel to your engine and keeping an eye on your gauges.

In other words, once you know things work, you only need to do awareness events and check in periodically to make sure they're still leading to sales.

6. Tinker with the Engine to Keep It Running Optimally (aka, Continuously Improve)

Once you have a productive and profitable marketing engine in place, it's better to tinker and scale than to build another engine.

After all, if you're going to do the work of building a keynote for a conference, then put in place some kind of opt-in download, a lead form handout, and a follow-up system.

You might as well see how many places you could give the same keynote to reach new audiences, right? To me, that makes a lot more sense than building all of that up, doing one talk, and then saying, "Okay, now we need to get into Facebook video."

But it's tempting for agencies to set something up and move on. That's because a lot of them do the same type of work for their clients: create websites, landing pages, or marketing funnels. Then start up the next one.

The problem with that approach? It tricks them into building more and more engines for *themselves*—but never actually putting one of them to proper use and getting results. They get stuck in "build" mode, not "fuel" mode.

Don't build multiple half-built marketing engines. I see a lot of people with a bunch of unproven and non-performing marketing engines. They have several landing pages with opt-ins tied to their website—but they don't invest any time or money into fueling their marketing engines with traffic. Or they have a bit of traffic with an opt-in, but no mechanism to convert those email signups into conversations.

I tell them the same thing I'm going to write here now: Your goal should be to build fewer, higher-performing engines—not more lower-performing ones.

Look again at the map in Exhibit 12 earlier in this chapter.

Let's say you've built an engine that drives email opt-ins from expert guest posts. If you can successfully use a multi-part email series, for example, to generate sales conversations, then you should attempt to scale and optimize that process before trying to build another marketing engine.

If you can then successfully earn a customer that is worth more than it costs in time and money to publish, you owe it to yourself to find the upper limit of that engine—the point at which it just doesn't work anymore.

Let's say you publish a few times, and you get some customers. What would happen if you doubled down on guest publishing? Could you get published monthly? What about weekly? What about daily? What systems and processes and contractors could you put in place to fuel your engine?

An agency I once worked with found themselves in this situation. They had discovered how to get about a client a week from guest publishing and were putting out about one article every two to three weeks.

They said, "Brent, this is working well, so what's next—should we start advertising on Facebook?" My response: "Have you exhausted all of your options for guest publishing? Are there any other bigger publishers or opportunities to publish more where you are already writing?"

When they told me there were at least a half dozen sites they had yet to build relationships with—and a few platforms that already wanted even more content—the answer was simple. Don't build something new and shiny, I told them. I advised my clients instead to work on scaling the engine that was already successful.

Why we resist "repeating ourselves." Listen—I understand the resistance.

Building marketing engines is the comfortable part, and trying and failing at different fuel activities—wasting money on poor performing ads or getting rejected by publishers—can get very uncomfortable. But while scaling a single engine demands laser-like focus and no small amount of discomfort, continually building new funnels creates an enormous sunk cost.

If you look at the different needs of a guest-blogging focused engine and a webinar-focused engine, for example, you'll find they have vastly different requirements. A client of mine gave a well-attended talk at a state conference. He got a dozen high-quality leads, and within a few weeks, he had closed his first deal.

He booked $24,000 in revenue from this single client, and if they stayed a loyal client beyond twelve months, that number would only go up. He estimated that at least four of the other leads would close within the next month or two. Possibly sooner—and the other leads would likely buy something within twelve to eighteen months.

But he was ready to move on to the next thing.

So I helped him realize that thirty other state-level associations across the country offered stages for him to go give the same talk—and that would likely give him similar results.

He'd need to get a testimonial from the association chair he worked with, create a pitch for his talk, build a list, make some phone calls, get rejected a few times, and take a few plane rides—but that seemed like a fair trade-off for the chance to generate five to six figures in business per stage.

The way the math worked, he only needed to get on three stages per year to double his business. That meant my client could ignore any and all "shiny objects" for the next couple of years and instead enjoy a more predictable, less sporadic business. He could optimize his engine and build momentum.

I recommend the same for you. Finish setting up your marketing engine, then focus on driving it "full out" and see how much you can get from it.

Marketing engines will go through five distinct stages on the path to scale:

Unproven: This is where all marketing engines start. You have an idea of a strategy to market your business. You'll invest some time and money to set up your engine and get traffic flowing.

Proven: If all goes well, you will generate your first lead—ideally a booked appointment on your calendar.

Repeatable: After your first lead, the next threshold to clear is whether you can generate a second lead from the same marketing engine.

Predictable: Once you've been able to repeat your success, the next stage requires you to get an idea of how many leads you'll generate from a given investment of time or money.

Scalable: The final stage of a high-performing marketing engine is being able to double or triple your inputs of time and money and get a matching increase in the outputs from your engine.

At some point, almost all marketing engines will find some upper ceiling when additional investments of time or money fail to get additional results. Only once it won't scale any more should you consider building a new one.

After all, you have in front of you an open road—and you've built a powerful "driving" machine. Does it make sense to get out there and give it all you've got?

Chapter Thirteen Take Aways to Get Rich In The Deep End

━━━━━━━━━━

◆ Marketing shouldn't be disconnected, random tactics. It should be an engine that you can put your foot on the gas and get a predictable and reliable result for your business.

◆ Your marketing system is like a car engine–needs a constant supply of fuel to get you where you want to go.

◆ You can't market your business one time and hope you are good to go for the next five years. Your engine needs to be fueled every week.

◆ Think of fuel for your marketing engine as *traffic sources*, ways that you can get eyeballs on your message with an investment of money or time.

◆ Awareness only matters if it drives conversations.

◆ No one ever paid their bills on awareness. They pay their bills from sales–and for agencies–sales happen in conversations. Every awareness activity MUST drive conversations.

◆ If you want people to contact you, give them what they want. Then sell them what they need.

◆ Remove the back and forth with scheduling leads on your calendar–and set boundaries for yourself to protect your time—use an appointment scheduling software to automate this for your lead funnels.

♦ Once you speak with a prospect, always schedule the next interaction. Never leave a meeting without a scheduled commitment to the next appointment.

♦ Strategy calls aren't about building your clients overall business or marketing strategy—it's a call to build the strategy for solving the problem at hand: setting a strategy to move forward with you as the solution.

♦ Every marketing engine has five stages: strategy, proven, repeatable, predictable, and scalable.

CHAPTER FOURTEEN

Heather Gives Her Talk

The conference center was packed.

The place was buzzing with energy; groups of people milled around, connecting, hugging, and chatting. You could tell the conference organizer—the top publisher in Heather's niche—had put a lot of effort into making everything "just so."

Heather stood in front of me, looking sharp. Her hair and makeup were done with a little more intensity than usual, and her black blazer and blouse pressed to a crisp edge. Inside, however, she was in turmoil. "Brent, I'm totally freaking out."

But although I heard the words coming out of Heather's mouth, her body language was saying something else entirely. She was absolutely radiating passion and purpose. For the first time, I could tell that Heather was truly dialed into what she was doing.

I tried to help her relax. "You've got this, Heather. You're prepared and you've done a ton of work. Now you just need to visualize how you want this to go—and let your intuition take care of the rest."

Heather shook out her arms and closed her eyes with a big exhale. "I know. I'm good."

As Heather opened her eyes, Amy walked up with Jake in tow—their bodies angled to make a show of hiding something behind their backs. Heather's face brightened as she exclaimed, "Hey, Amy! Jake! I didn't expect to see you here!"

Jake spoke first in his slow Southern drawl. "Well, you know, Heather, Amy called me. She said you were gettin' up on stage for the first time. And I thought, Well, butter my butt and call me a biscuit! She's talking in Denver? How could I miss it? Besides, I didn't think it was right to let you get up there without one of these!"

Jake pulled a large chef's hat from behind his back and placed it ceremoniously on Heather's head. We all let out booming laughs. "Well, bless your heart, Heather," Jake said. "I do reckon you're as pretty as a peach."

That's when I stepped in with a plan of my own. "Stand back a bit for me, Heather. I want to get a full picture of your getup."

"Brent you're kidding me. You can't possibly expect me to wear this thing."

I made a show of looking her up and down, like a fashion designer dressing a model.

"Hmmm. Heather, maybe you're right.

"You know, you're just about ready to own your market. But I think there's one thing missing. Maybe if we trade the hat."

That was Amy's cue. "Heather," she said, "let's see if we can swap that jacket out for an upgrade."

With a flourish, Amy produced something from behind her own back—Heather's vibrant Versace jacket, the one with the bright primary colors and Vogue magazine covers.

Heather was speechless. "How did you—?"

Amy smiled. "Brent mentioned you had said something about the jacket at one point—and how you wished business could be more fun.

"So I sent that wonderful husband of yours a message. And he snuck it out of your closet last week so we could get it cleaned and pressed without you knowing. It's time for you to really own your market, Heather. And that means being you."

I removed the chef's hat—"I don't think you'll be needing this to stand out anymore, Heather"—and opened the jacket so she could put it on.

Heather did a spin. She instinctively buttoned the top button and smoothed the jacket's front. Then she stretched her arms out to her sides and slightly tugged on the jacket sleeves to straighten them out.

She was beaming. "I'm going to review my presentation one last time and collect myself in the speaker lounge. I go on in a couple of hours, but before I do… Guys, thank you. Knowing you're here will give me the added boost I need. And the jacket—what a nice touch. And Brent, no matter how this goes for me, I want to thank you.

"The last few months have been the most fun I've had in my business for years. I feel like I have something truly unique for once. I can't even tell you how much I appreciate what you've done for me. Thank you."

"Of course, Heather," I said. "You're welcome. Thank you for doing the work and being coachable. You would be surprised at how many people actually aren't. Thank you for trusting the process."

And with that, Heather disappeared into the crowd.

Top-Shared Guide

Amy, Jake, and I filed into the main ballroom and found seats as close to the front as we could manage. I glanced around the room to take an inventory. From the way the room was laid out, I estimated there were about a thousand business coaches and consultants seated in the rows of chairs facing the stage. Probably one of the larger conferences in the niche.

Amy leaned in and said, "Brent, I can't believe Heather got booked by these guys so quickly! Whatever you did, it worked!"

I replied, "You know, Amy, your case study and connections did more of the work than you think. I just got Heather on the right track to leverage what you both had already done so well."

Just then the ballroom dimmed, and the stage lit up. An energetic gentleman in his mid-forties took the stage with a mic in his hand, and the conference—focusing on helping business coaches and consultants build million-dollar practices—was underway.

We heard from an experienced motivational coach about mindset. Then from another about scalable business models and how to create a leveraged practice.

It occurred to me that these speakers were seasoned professionals. Their talks were dialed in—I could tell that each had not only practiced relentlessly but had probably delivered the same speech a dozen or more times from live stages.

They were tough acts to follow, and I won't lie—I was worried that Heather might have been in over her head.

Soon it was the moment of truth. The emcee stepped back onto the stage and rallied up the crowd into a roaring round of applause. Jake leaned over Amy and tapped my leg. He motioned to the side of the stage and pointed—there was Heather, standing behind the curtain.

Jake whispered, "She's got gumption!"

And with that, the emcee introduced Heather while glancing at his confidence monitor to rattle off the proof points Heather and I worked on.

 **Success happens at the intersection of money, interest, and results.**

"Next up—a fast-rising star in our world, owner of an award-winning digital agency focused on helping the top coaches in the world grow their businesses online, as featured in Coaching Today and Guru Academy. And most recently, she wrote a stellar piece on our own website that quickly became the top shared guide among our community. So it's with great pleasure and excitement that I welcome Heather Carlyle to the stage!"

Heather jogged out from stage left in, yes, her Versace jacket. As the crowd welcomed her to the room with a nice big round of applause, she shook the emcee's hand and walked to a small table to grab the presentation remote.

I could see a nervous edge as she picked up the device. I don't think anyone who didn't know her would have seen it, but there was a bit of a shake in her hand. She must have been on fire with nerves and energy. But there was nothing I could say or do to help her—it was all on her.

As Heather stepped back to the center of the stage with her clicker, she took a deep breath and began. "Thanks, John. It's so great to be here. What an amazing start to the day. Everyone having a great time so far?"

There were some nods and a few yeses from the audience. A serious look came over Heather's face. "Look. This is my first time up on a stage like this. If this is going to work over the next forty minutes, I'm going to need more than that. So I'll ask again: is everyone having a great time so far?"

The room lit up with excitement as people started to hoot and holler. As the energy died down, Heather affected a kind of stage whisper. "Look, I need a favor. See, I know the conference organizers are down the hall right now. And I want to impress them and get invited back next year to speak—so I need you to be on my team and help me make this happen.

"And if you do this for me, I'll give you twenty times the value I was originally planning. Is that a deal?"

A few audience members shouted, "Yeah!"

Amy tilted her head and looked over at me. I shrugged my shoulders, "This is all her. I had nothing to do with this."

Heather went on. "Okay, on the count of three I want everyone here to leap to your feet and clap and applaud like your team just won the Super Bowl, the World Series, and the NBA Finals all at once. Scream like your kid just graduated from elementary, high school, and college on the same day. Make everyone down there in the hotel lobby jealous that they can't get into this room, okay?

"One, two, three!"

And with that, the entire room stood up on their feet and let out an enormous roar. They stomped their feet and yelled and screamed and whistled. And if I hadn't known who was up on stage, I would have thought it was a rock concert.

I'm not ashamed to say Amy, Jake, and I lost ourselves in the moment too, and just about screamed ourselves hoarse. When the energy subsided and everyone took their seats, Heather said, "Wow. Thank you for delivering your end of the bargain. I guess now it's my turn."

Heather stepped to the middle of the stage and asked a question. "Who here has an assistant or VA of some kind?"

Almost the entire room raised their hands.

"Okay, keep your hands raised if your assistant is amazing."

A few hands shrunk back down.

"Now, how many of you let your assistant market and sell for you?"

More hands went down.

"What about deliver your programs and services for you?"

Most of the hands went down, and only a few stayed up.

"Okay, now of those people with their hands still in the air. How many of you have assistants that work twenty-four hours a day, seven days a week, 365 days a year—with no vacation, sick pay, or complaints. And get paid about six cents an hour to do their job?"

The few hands remaining disappeared and a wave of laughter rippled through the room.

Heather had found her groove.

"Ladies and gentlemen, I'd like to introduce you to your new personal assistant. This PA can attract high-quality leads, sell them on your programs and services, accept unlimited credit card orders simultaneously, deliver thousands of hours of content without breaking a sweat, and run your entire business while you go do other things like sitting on the beach drinking fruity cocktails, or spending time with family."

Heather clicked her slide deck forward. With a dramatic reveal, the two large screens behind her both read:

Your Website

Heather took a moment to pause.

"Over the next half hour or so, I want to change your mind-set about your website and the online marketing systems you build for your coaching practice. And by the end of this presentation, I want you to start thinking of your website as not an online brochure, but as the most powerful and relentless member of your team that can help you grow, scale, and leverage your time to unbelievable levels of success."

The audience was leaning into Heather's every word. I glanced around the room and saw hundreds of people flipping to new pages in their notebooks and shifting in their seats to listen intently.

And I thought to myself, "Well done, Heather. You've got them hooked."

The Pitch

It should come as no surprise that Heather delivered the goods. She told stories. She built tension using a three-act structure. She shared case studies and testimonials. And she threw in enough gold nuggets and social proof to never worry about being a credible go-to in the business coach market again.

But then it was time for her to make her pitch to acquire leads and start on a path to conversations. She had been nervous about it, so I almost reflexively held my breath. We had come up with a simple framework that she packaged into a download. And she had set up a text message opt-in service that would capture a phone number and then push to an email-based opt-in page.

But would it work?

Heather started in. "One of the tools I've built is a simple planner that will help you map out the different business functions your website can serve for you. It will help you get more leverage out of your business. Is this something that would be useful for everyone?"

And then she paused.

"Real quick show of hands. Who here would like to get access to that planner?"

She handled it like an old pro!

"Awesome. Just before today's event, I set up a service to help you download that tool. To get it, all you have to do is text the word *leverage* to the number you see on the screen."

Almost in unison, hundreds of audience members pulled out their phones and started requesting Heather's lead magnet. She must have captured three hundred leads or more. And when it looked like everyone was close to done, Heather wrapped up her pitch.

"Now, because I think you're all so awesome, I'm also happy to review your Leverage Plan with you one on one. For those that decided to take me up on this free tool, there's a link in the download email to schedule a time on my calendar.

"My only request is that you put in the work and do the planner first so I can be of best help to you. And if you haven't downloaded the tool yet, make sure to do that now if you're interested in that one-on-one call."

 **Becoming an authority in your market has all sorts of benefits. More leads. Faster sales. Higher prices. It's worth the investment.**

Then she finished strong with a personal story about what it meant for her to be able to help Amy achieve leverage in her business, then a thank you and some final information on how audience members could get in touch with her.

But to tell the truth, I didn't really hear that part. My mind had wandered—thinking about Heather's journey to this event.

In just a few short months, she had gone from being just another agency owner to a sought-after expert for business coaches. And between the work she'd been doing in her market, the endorsements she had earned with her publishers, and her success on stage—she was no longer going to have any trouble getting noticed.

After all, she owned her market now. And she was on her way to building the business of her dreams.

Here We Go Again

Amy, Jake, and I stood nearby in a corner of the conference hall. Heather had been talking to audience members for twenty minutes or more. As luck would have it, she had been scheduled right before lunch, so the ten or so people still in line had plenty of time.

Jake turned to me and said, "Brent, you've really got this down to a science. Helping people become the go-to in their market. You did it for me, you did it for Heather—I bet you do it for a lot of people."

"I appreciate that Jake," I said. "But the credit goes to folks like you and Heather. When Heather started, she swore she'd never get on stage. And then just a few months later, it happened. And she followed through.

"It takes a lot of courage for people like you and Heather to do what you do. I just help get you started in the right direction."

Heather's line finally dissipated, and she slowly walked over to our group with her eyes wide and her arms stretched out to the sides.

She was overjoyed. "That was insane I can't even believe what just happened. I've already got handshakes on a couple of new deals. And one woman told me that she had to work with me because I was the obvious choice for business coach marketing."

I congratulated her. "I guess the question, Heather, is where do you go from here?"

Heather thought for a second and replied with a laugh. "Well, I don't know. I'm certainly not short for leads right now.

"Oh, by the way, I forgot to mention to you, Jake! There was so much excitement before the conference I didn't tell you—a restaurant called EMA to ask about working with us and I referred them to you."

A big smile came across my face. "Now we know things must be turning around. You're now passing off leads. Who could have imagined that happening just a few short months ago?"

Jake laughed. "I appreciate that a whole lot, Heather. Now, here's an 'oh, by the way' for you. I've been thinking about launching a course for restaurant owners—and maybe even coaching some of the ones who can't afford my services. I'd love to talk to you about it. After all, you're now the authority in this market."

We chuckled and said our goodbyes, leaving Heather to enjoy the rest of the conference. As I walked to the parking lot, I checked my email. There were a dozen or so messages in my inbox, but one caught my eye:

"Brent, I'm so frustrated with running my agency. I'm thinking of getting into a different business entirely. It's like no one values what I do and I can't consistently find clients. Can you hop on a call? I'm happy to pay you for your time."

"Here we go," I thought. "The adventure begins again."

And I paused for a moment in gratitude, thankful for all of the agency owners I've been lucky enough to meet over the years. Some ended up ignoring their market and faltering after our time together, but others succeeded beyond their wildest dreams—and all because one day they took a chance on working with me to own their market.

But what about you? Are you ready to take that chance?

Chapter Fourteen Take Aways to Get Rich In The Deep End

♦ When you're in front of your audience, you become the absolute best version of yourself. Audiences don't connect with average–the connect with outstanding. Be the most outstanding version of yourself.

♦ When it comes to being memorable, it's always the crazy ideas that end up working the best. Dressing up as a panda, having a lightsaber battle in front of 300 people, building a life size cutout of myself to unveil on stage as my new business card. When you get that "crazy thought" of how you could stand out in your market, don't say no, make it even crazier.

♦ Engage your audience by enrolling them in your idea. Make them co-conspirators to your cause.

♦ Pitch your offer as a way to help. A way to serve. When you do that, you'll never come across as salesy.

♦ When your market puts you out in front–whether on a podcast interview, stage, virtual panel, article, or any other form of awareness–you instantly become an authority. An influencer. Someone who will now be sought after by people looking to solve the problems you talk about.

♦ Never underestimate the power of authority in your niche.

CONCLUSION

A New Way

I believe there are two ways to run a digital agency: the old way and the new way. The old way is how agencies have operated for decades, but the *new way* can be embraced by any agency owner. No level of competition or innovation will ever put an expiration date on this concept.

When you run an agency the old way, the priority is "staff augmentation"—someone forms a company, collects a group of highly skilled individuals, and then hangs out a shingle that says, "Open for business."

Clients then buy the talent of that collection of individuals. Scopes of work for fixed price projects and hourly retainers are involved. In some cases, clients even "rent" these folks full-time for projects or needs.

The old way makes agency owners believe that *any* business is a potential client. As long as a lead has a need for the agency's services—and the ability to pay for them—the company is past the first hurdle.

Consequently, the measure of an hour becomes the central factor in how these agencies operate.

These agency owners resist the idea of choosing a market or "niching down" in fear that they will be forgoing opportunities outside their niche. After all, they might have to start saying no to potential clients they think would be a good fit. (Anybody with a checkbook, right?)

 **Dressing up as a panda, having a lightsaber battle in front of 300 people, building a life size cutout of myself to unveil on stage as my new business card. When you get that "crazy thought" of how you could stand out in your market, don't say no, make it even crazier.**

Listen, I get it. There are some advantages to the old way of running an agency. Being able to accept a wide range of clients makes you feel busier, for example. But there are downsides.

Generalist agencies are extraordinarily challenging to scale. Each new client requires a lot of learning—and often breaks processes because the project is different from what the agency has done before.

When you offer an extensive complement of services to a broad range of clients, the skills on your team end up varying wildly. That makes calculating your agency's production capacity an extraordinary feat, usually only possible with the most skilled project manager.

Generalist agencies also become susceptible to working with "whale clients"—massive retainer-based jobs that create an outsized dependency on a single account.

Nobody talks much about internal whales, but they exist too. What if individual team members become critical to your success? You won't be able to fire them if they're a bad fit for your organization or lay them off in a downturn, and being held hostage is no fun.

Now, if you're reading this and you recognize yourself, you might be thinking, *"Relax, Brent. I've got this."*

Well, I don't want to make you defensive, but the outlook ain't great.

I've interviewed hundreds of agencies owners for my YouTube channel and podcast, The Digital Agency Show.[20] I've talked to more than a few generalist agencies that prided themselves on being "above any one niche." Too many of them share with me—just a short time later—that they lost a couple of accounts, had a bad month or two and ended up laying off 80% of their staff.

The saddest part? They all say the same things: "The economy is terrible right now." "Referrals have just dried up." "There are too many DIY options." And so on.

It breaks my heart because the truth is that agencies who embrace the new way of doing business—the *right* way—don't struggle like this. The new way of running a digital agency is fundamentally different from the old way. It's about refusing to build a business around the staff augmentation model—put bodies in seats, have those bodies produce hours of work. The new way means building a business around achieving a very specific result for only a certain type of client.

When you can do that, and you can prove that you can reproduce that result for more than one client, your business will become infinitely scalable. So believe me when I say I sincerely hope you use the 5-A framework.

Strategically select your *Audience.*

Choose *Awareness* channels that leverage the power of one-to-many marketing.

Identify the top problems and opportunities that will *Attract* your audience to engage with you.

Establish your *Authority* by sharing real-world results and third-party endorsements.

And build a system to *Acquire* new leads and clients—and stop leaving business up to chance.

 **Owning your market brings respect, desirability, authority, process, demand, scale, predictability, clarity, and simplicity.**

You'll talk about what you do in places where your ideal client hangs out. They'll become attracted to you because you understand their problems better than they do themselves. That will put them in mind to learn about your proven and predictable solution to their challenges.

You'll continuously build awareness of your agency, and that awareness will help you regularly attract and acquire new leads. You'll create systems in your business that can operate like clockwork—because you won't be reinventing the wheel with each new project.

And because you can have systems, you'll put people in place that can run them. For once, you won't be the main bottleneck in your business.

Over time, you'll compile unique intellectual property, which will add value to your business beyond the billable hour. Instead of being beholden to team members with exceptional skills and experience, your business will live on through team turnover or inevitable market fluctuations.

Your processes will become assets. Your client list and email list will become assets. Your intellectual property will become an asset—as will your unique market knowledge and the connections you've built up. Finally, your engine to attract, convert, and deliver results to your market will become yet another asset.

As these assets build, your enterprise will grow, and instead of a job, you'll have a business that is more valuable than the time you invest each day or week. Best of all, you'll solve more interesting problems. You won't break your back with each new project—and then wonder where the next client is coming from. Instead, you'll start to solve problems around scaling your agency or building a team culture, productizing your services, and so on.

In other words, you'll have options, and in this book, options are a synonym for freedom. Here's why I wrote Get Rich In The Deep End: I want you to achieve freedom in your business and life.

I believe that when you get to *choose* how you grow your business and determine the way you scale, then you have freedom. Maybe you want to make a lot more money. Great. One of my clients netted over $100,000 for himself in the first six months that he ran his agency the *new way*. (Compare that to before, when his agency booked about $500,000 annually but he took home only about $30,000 of it.)

Maybe you want to spend time doing something other than your business. Awesome. Another client of mine chooses to operate her business for fewer than twenty hours per week so she can tend to her daughter's medical needs.

Maybe you want to become a sought-after expert in your market—and have people pay you for your content and expertise. I have a client who gets paid thousands of dollars for every keynote and workshop he delivers in his market. That's more than some of his services used to earn him.

Or maybe you want to work with clients that bring you more happiness and fulfillment. Yet another of my clients has chosen to work only with businesses that support renewable and environmentally sustainable causes.

Here's the point of all of this: I want you to be able to take control of your future and enjoy the fruits of your labor. I want you to build wealth and excitement and value and become a positive force of change in the world.

I want you to *Own Your Market.*

There is an old way to run a digital agency: anyone can be your client and you'll survive on referrals.

And there is a new way…

Get ready to take the plunge into the deep end of the niche pool. You define a narrow set of problems and you become the highly paid specialist to solve those problems for anyone in the world.

That's how you niche your business, own your market, and audaciously scale your agency.

That's how you get rich!

Heather Comes Full Circle

Later that night, Heather was still there in the hotel restaurant, working hard. She had wanted to go back across town to EMA, but she'd been so busy following up on leads that she had decided just to make a night of it.

She'd been flipping through email after email from attendees. A few people weren't able to find appointments on her calendar, so— despite some concern about being able to handle so many leads—she opened up more spots on her schedule.

When it rains, it pours, she thought, and motioned to her server that she was ready for the bill. She had also spent some time considering her next move.

She'd already had plenty of additional publishing opportunities, but now the same people who put on the conference wanted her to do a webinar, and maybe even a small in-person workshop at an out-of-state event in a few months.

All in all, she was pretty grateful as she packed up. What a day. But then a voice shook her out of her reverie.

"Heather Carlyle, right?"

"That's me," she said, but Heather didn't quite recognize the man introducing himself.

"Gary Rogers. We met years ago at a digital marketing conference. I heard your talk today—it was fantastic."

Heather blushed.

"Sure! Gary, nice to see you here. I remember now. What are you doing here?"

"Oh, you know. I've been thinking about getting into business coaching. My agency isn't doing that great, and I can't figure out how to grow it. I wish I could get the kind of exposure that you do at EMA."

Heather chuckles and softly smiled. "Gary, I know what you're going through. Just a few months ago, I was right where you are today."

"Really?"

"You have no idea. We almost closed our doors. Well, maybe that wouldn't have happened. But I was just a couple of days away from laying off a bunch of people."

Then Heather's eyes lit up with the memory of a conversation she'd had months ago. "Gary, I may have something you'd be interested in. Let me see if I still have it."

Heather rummaged around in her bag. Eventually, she found what she was looking for. "Gary, this rumpled old thing is a business card. Someone once gave it to me—this very one. And now I want to give it to you. A phone call to the number on this card right here was what started to turn things around for me. And it's possible it could do the same for you."

Gary looked puzzled. "You mean this guy is your secret? And you're just giving that information out?"

Heather smiled. She remembered all the work she had done since calling that number. All of the sleepless nights, the stress of choosing her market, the rejection along the way, and the fear she had to overcome to put herself out there. She thought about how, earlier that year, she'd been a nobody in this market—and now she was a somebody.

"Well, Gary, it's a little more complicated than that, but Brent helped me a ton, and hopefully, he can help you too. He taught me that it was never about my market or about niching down. It was about allowing myself to become the entrepreneur I always wanted to be. About going all-in on being Heather—and about pushing through when I didn't want to do the work to get there.

"But you don't have to worry about any of that right now. You can start by just giving him a call."

Gary was astounded. "Wow, thanks, Heather. I guess I'll see you around. Maybe from that big stage back there. Who knows? One day I just might."

Heather nodded. "You know what, Gary? I bet you will."

About the Author

Brent Weaver is on a mission to help 10,000 digital agency owners achieve freedom in business and life by helping them own their market.

Brent is the founder and CEO of UGURUS, a business training and education company dedicated to this mission. He also hosts one of the leading podcasts in the business niche—The Digital Agency Show.

Brent is in partnership with UnlimitedWP—a scalable white label WordPress development team to help digital agencies grow without all the headaches of hiring and managing people. He is also a Brand Ambassador for Cloudways, a WordPress hosting company, helping them evangelize their platform.

When Brent isn't working with agency owners around the globe, he enjoys going on date nights with his wife Emily and biking at the local skatepark with his two sons.

REFERENCES

Notes

1 *Oxford English Dictionary*, "own." https://www.lexico.com/en/definition/own.

2 Deming, William Edwards. *The New Economics for Industry, Government, Education*. 2nd ed. MIT Press, 2000, p. 92.

3 Vaynerchuk, Gary. "Content Is King, but Context Is God." Gary Vaynerchuk (website). 2015. https://www.garyvaynerchuk.com/content-is-king-but-context-is-god/.

4 Aristotle. *Metaphysics* 8.6. In MIT Classics. Translated by W. D. Ross. http://classics.mit.edu/Aristotle/metaphysics.8.viii.html.

5 Gladwell, Malcolm. *The Tipping Point: How Little Things Can Make a Big Difference*. Little, Brown, & Company, 2006.

6 Pressfield, Steven. *The War of Art: Break Through the Blocks and Win Your Inner Creative Battles*. Black Irish Entertainment LLC, 2002.

7 Clement, J. "Percentage of Global Population Accessing the Internet from 2005 to 2018, by Market Maturity." Statista. January 9, 2019. https://www.statista.com/statistics/209096/share-of-internet-users-in-the-total-world-population-since-2006/.

[8] Lynkova, Darina. "The Surprising Reality of How Many Emails Are Sent Per Day." Tech Jury. April 22, 2019. https://techjury.net/stats-about/how-many-emails-are-sent-per-day/#gref.

[9] Marr, Bernard. "How Much Data Do We Create Every Day? The Mind-Blowing Stats Everyone Should Read." Forbes. May 21, 2018. https://www.forbes.com/sites/bernardmarr/2018/05/21/how-much-data-do-we-create-every-day-the-mind-blowing-stats-everyone-should-read/#2c1614ca60ba.

[10] Harari, Yuval Noah. *Sapiens: A Brief History of Humankind.* HarperCollins, 2015.

[11] Weaver, Brent. "Never Say WordPress When Selling a Web Design Project." SpeckyBoy. November 18, 2016. https://speckyboy.com/never-say-wordpress/

[12] Pressfield, Steven. *Nobody Wants to Read Your Sh*t: Why That Is and What You Can Do About It.* Black Irish Entertainment LLC, 2016.

[13] Weaver, "Never Say WordPress."

[14] Godin, Seth. *The Dip: A Little Book That Teaches You When to Quit (and When to Stick).* Portfolio, 2007.

[15] *Lexico,* "authority." https://www.lexico.com/en/definition/authority.

[16] Weaver, "Never Say WordPress."

[17] DeWitt, Ken. "Tired of Repeating Yourself to Your Employees?" EOS Worldwide. June 1, 2017. https://blog.eosworldwide.com/blog/tired-repeating-yourself-employees.

[18] *Latin-English Dictionary,* "repetitio est mater studiorum in English." Glosbe. https://glosbe.com/la/en/repetitio%20est%20mater%20studiorum.

[19] Coleman, Joey. "Joey Coleman First 100 Days." Executive Speakers Bureau. September 6, 2018. https://www.youtube.com/watch?v=34253Mj5wxA.

[20] Weaver, Brent. *The Digital Agency Show.* UGURUS. https://ugurus.com/podcast/.